MACHINE EMBROIDERY:
stitch
techniques

MACHINE EMBROIDERY:
stitch techniques

*Valerie Campbell-Harding
and
Pamela Watts*

B. T. BATSFORD LTD., LONDON

Acknowledgement

We would like to thank our friends, colleagues and students for their support and for so generously allowing us to photograph their work.

Our thanks to: Sara and Ian MacPherson of Madeira Threads for their gift of threads; Whaleys of Bradford and Vilene Products for their gift of fabrics; Pfaff for the loan of a machine and for their help; Elna and New Home for the loan of machines; all our machine dealers for their help and patience; Geoffrey Wheeler for developing and printing the photographs.

The illustrations, drawings and diagrams are the work of the authors unless otherwise stated.

© Valerie Campbell-Harding and Pamela Watts 1989
First published 1989
Reprinted 1992

ISBN 0 7134 5797 X

Typeset by
Lasertext Limited, Stretford, Manchester
and printed in Great Britain by
The Bath Press, Bath

for the publishers
B. T. Batsford Ltd
4 Fitzhardinge Street,
London W1H 0AH

Contents

Introduction 6

1 Running stitch 9

2 Whip stitch 38

3 Cable stitch 52

4 Zigzag stitch 60

5 Satin stitch 75

6 Further developments of
stitch techniques 95

7 Exploring colour 108

8 Combining different
stitches 110

9 Interpreting your drawings
and designs 124

Troubleshooting 140

What to look for when
choosing a sewing
machine 141

Further reading 142

Suppliers 143

Index 144

Introduction

The words 'machine embroidery' attract a variety of reactions. Some people immediately think of commercially produced motifs, or assume that it is the machine which makes the patterns. Others feel that it is an inferior craft to hand embroidery.

A glance at the contents of this book will show that we are not dealing with commercial patterns, and that machine embroidery is not in opposition to hand techniques – as embroiderers, we use whatever tools will give the results we want. For hand stitching the fabric is still and you move the needle; with machining the needle is still and you move the fabric. We may be biased, but we believe that the machine has endless potential. You have a strong, untiring motor to help you, sophisticated and precise engineering at your command, and the ability to produce exactly the style of embroidery which appeals to you. It is fun, relaxing and exhilarating all at the same time.

If you are a newcomer to machine embroidery, your early efforts may fall short of your expectations. When learning to drive, you can make the car move but would hardly tackle Spaghetti Junction on your first outing. A beginner can pick up a violin and make sounds, but would not expect to play a concerto. Everyone will tell you that practice makes perfect. Although we all know this is true, we hope to make your practice pleasurable and the results exciting. Familiarity with your machine is all-important, and confidence grows in leaps and bounds as you realize that your machine *does* do what you want – it is a real partnership. In our teaching, we sometimes hear, 'my machine does not like that', as if the machine had an opinion on the matter! Of course it does, in a way, but it is only saying that it cannot do what you intended. Perhaps you have asked the impossible. Your machine does not scream and shout – it just quietly breaks the thread or makes a strange noise, so that you can remedy the situation and continue stitching.

We hope you will keep this book propped up by your machine as a teaching aid. Each stitch technique is fully explained for the beginner and, for the more experienced machine embroiderer, there are many ideas for developing and combining the techniques. Throughout the book we have avoided reference to particular makes or models of machines. We have aimed to give guidance which applies to the vast majority of sewing machines in use today. This approach is based on our teaching experience, where it is usual to have a group of students and no two machines alike. Between us, we own three Berninas, two Singers, a New Home, and an Elna, and have used Pfaff, Riccar, Viking and Frister Rossman machines. We have tried out the stitch techniques on all these models. Some machines or models are easier for certain techniques or give better results, but these are usually minor points, and we have tried to include all the variations necessary to enable you to work through the techniques and ideas. We have assumed that you are familiar with your sewing machine for dressmaking and household sewing, if not for embroidery. We do not, therefore, give information on how to thread the machine, change the needle or use the basic functions. We do recommend regular reading of your machine manual, as there are numerous little points you may have missed or forgotten about. Our other recommendation is to make a friend of your dealer. If you have problems or queries about your machine, take your stitch samples with you and he will then understand what you are trying to do and be able to help you.

Your machine has the built-in potential for embroidery, even if you did not know that when you bought it. People are amazed when they see the range of textures that can be produced on an ordinary domestic sewing machine. A builder working at a machine embroiderer's house, on seeing embroidery being produced, enquired, 'Does that machine do ordinary sewing as well?' The answer, of course, is yes, but they do so many wonderful and exciting things too.

Fabrics

Most embroiderers have a selection of fabrics, but we all seem to choose calico for practising machine embroidery. Although it is a good choice, there are many other fabrics which are equally suitable and we suggest you experiment with a wide range. Collect together pieces of different types so that you can see how the nature of the fabric completely changes the appearance of a line of stitching. Try felt, paper, net, pelmet – weight interfacing (such as Vilene or Pellon), leather, velvet and satin. A little ingenuity makes the list even longer (include stitching on ribbons or knitting). If you have pieces of the old quilting wadding, which has a papery surface layer, try machining lines or a grid pattern to see the stitching sink into the surface. (The more modern polyester waddings can catch on the presser foot and the feed dog, so it is as well to avoid these for the moment.) Dark fabrics make a change, and if you are using pale fabrics like calico, you can paint, sponge or print on the fabric before you start. An expanse of plain fabric can be very off-putting, and even coloured lines with a felt-tip pen give you a starting point. Take a little piece of sponge, a pot of fabric paint and dab areas of colour on to the fabric before stitching. The result will look much more exciting. Many more ideas are given in the following chapters on using different fabrics, printing and stitching together.

Threads

Wonderful threads, specially made for machine embroidery, can now be bought from specialist shops or by mail order. There are rayon and cotton threads in a wide colour range, plus shaded, variegated and lovely metallic threads. You can, of course, use any machine sewing thread, as well as others intended for hand embroidery, lace or other crafts. Although it may be tempting to use up old reels for practice, do try each technique with the thread you intend to use, as the different types and thicknesses affect the tension, as well as the way the stitch will look. In addition, old thread, especially cotton, becomes dry and brittle and will undoubtedly break, which is annoying. Store your threads away from sunlight, preferably in a covered container.

Machine threads come in various thicknesses, and the higher the number the thinner the thread. Many machines, particularly the European ones, prefer the finer threads, but you will soon discover which suit your machine. The manual may advise using the same thread on the top and in the bobbin. Although this is sensible for dressmaking, a more flexible approach is needed for embroidery. If you are using a shiny rayon thread on top you may find it best to use cotton on the bobbin. Please do not wind one colour on top of another on the bobbin as this really does lead to disaster when embroidering. Buy more bobbins whenever you can; you will always need more.

Using 'tricky' threads

The most economical way to buy machine embroidery threads is to get the large 1,000-metre reels. These are wound on a tube and do not have an edge to the reel. Unfortunately, embroiderers find that the thread unravels, catches on the spool pin and breaks. This can easily be overcome by keeping the thread at mid-spool height so that it cannot tighten on the base. Some machines have two spool pins with a hole in the top of one, through which you can put the thread. The carrying handle on the top of some models has a wire loop at the back for the same purpose. Your dealer may sell a gadget to keep the thread up, or you can tape a bodkin to the back of the machine with the eye as high as possible, between the spool pin and the threading system, to take the thread. A horizontal spool pin is usually trouble-free, so enquire whether your machine will take one. One of the easiest remedies is to check whether your bobbins will fit on the spool pin. If they do, wind a bobbin with the thread, using it on the top. Place a reel of cotton on top of the bobbin to add tension and to stop it leaping up and down. In spite of all precautions, some top threads do snap easily. Assuming they are not brittle and that you have threaded the machine correctly, the best remedy is to loosen the top tension, bit by bit, until you are confident it will not break. If fraying of the thread occurs, omit the last thread holder before the needle, particularly if this is tight. With the thicker threads and particularly the metal threads, loosen the top tension still more and use a larger needle.

Preparing your machine

Before you begin any machine embroidery, do check that your machine is clean and in perfect working order (see 'Care of your machine' on page 140).

The box system

For each different stitch technique, You will find the basic guidelines for setting up your machine printed in a box like this one. We hope you will use this as a checklist until familiarity and confidence make the settings second nature to you. Variations on the settings may be suggested for particular effects, but these will be explained in the text.

1 *Running stitch, showing the effect of different stitch lengths using thick, thin, smooth and rough threads. These samples were worked with the fabric framed and the presser foot on.*

1 Running Stitch

Starting to stitch

The first part of this chapter describes running stitch with the presser foot on and the feed dog up. A single line of machining is so familiar that it is easy to overlook the potential of this technique. Thread your machine with a favourite colour and select a normal stitch length, just as you would for dressmaking or household sewing. Choose a firm cotton fabric, and you may wish to put the fabric in a ring frame. This will make the fabric easier to manoeuvre, but you will have to remove the presser foot, and replace it, each time you put the frame under the needle. The frame is used so that the fabric is resting on the bed of the machine. Work rows close together,

Top tension	-- Normal
Bobbin tension	-- Normal
Presser foot	-- On
Feed dog	-- Up
Stitch length	-- Very short to long
Stitch width	-- 0
Fabric	-- Framed
Needle size	-- 90

backwards and forwards, until you have a solid band of stitching. If a line wobbles and the fabric shows, go back and fill in with another row. Try as many different types of thread as you can find. Fit a larger needle, size 100 or even 110, and use top stitching thread made for dressmaking, thin crochet thread, silk twist, metallic threads or the new wool and rayon floss machine threads. Change the stitch length from very short up to the maximum on different bands. Massed lines look so much more interesting showing the constrast of matt and shiny

2 *Left* Running *stitch used over torn pieces of organza and of an oil painting, both to decorate and to secure the pieces.*

3 Below *Stitching on different fabrics to see the effect. Velvet and polythene bag over wadding.*

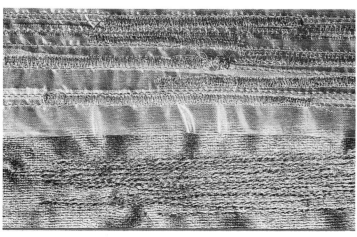

threads, with the different stitch lengths giving ridged textures. This is an excellent way of learning about threads with the added bonus of producing a really solid fabric which would be practical on cuffs, belts or bags.

Fabrics

Just as massed lines of stitching alter the feel of the fabric, the fabric itself alters the nature of the stitch. Using the same normal machine settings, stitch on fabrics which have very different textures. Alter the stitch lengths as before, aiming for many lines together, then spaces to let the fabric show through. Be really inventive and machine solid bands on fur fabric or over patterned fabric to add stripes of a new colour.

Stabilizers

Thin fabrics may need a backing or stabilizer underneath them to give body and to control puckering while you stitch. Paper or tear-away backing can be used, and both can be torn away from the unstitched areas when finished. They

do alter the feel and drape of the fabric, so you may prefer to use two layers of fabric together. Felt or domette can be used as a backing, which is very interesting as the stitching will sink into the fabric.

Experimenting with layers

Although your stitching is, for the moment, quite simple, aim to experiment with as many fabrics and effects as you can, to broaden your approach to the basic materials. This will be invaluable experience later on. Tear little pieces of paper and stitch them on to fabric in layers. Cut or tear sheer fabrics and nets and stitch them on to paper – not just plain paper, but pages from colour magazines, or your own hand-made or printed papers. Polythene can be placed over bundles of thin threads or textured slub yarns, with lines of machining to secure them. Most of all, enjoy the process of handling fabrics and papers and machining on them.

4 *Stitching in different directions using a variegated thread.*
Top right to hold down loose threads.
Bottom right to hold down pieces of fabric.
Bottom left on sprayed pelmet-weight interfacing.
Top left the stitching was sprayed with gold over loose squares of paper, and extra squares of stitched fabric were piled up at the intersections.

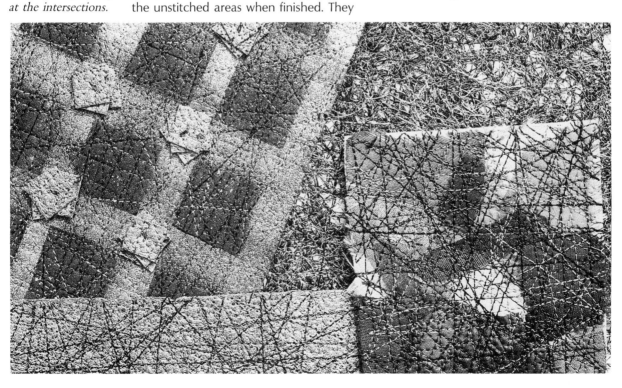

Stitching in different directions

As well as machining in straight lines you can, of course, stitch vertically, horizontally, diagonally or in any direction you wish. This is effective using a shiny thread with a long stitch length, as the light catches the thread in different directions, changing the tone. Pelmet-weight interfacing such as Vilene (Pellon) is a wonderful material to experiment with, as it is firm enough to be moved around easily. It also takes paint and dye very well. Combine these qualities to gain confidence in producing your own patterns. Lay some strips of paper, fabric or sticky tape on a piece of pelmet interfacing, arranging them to form a grid or diamond pattern. Sponge or spray fabric paint on to the material (don't forget to protect nearby surfaces). Car spray paints are an easy and quick way of doing this. Remove the strips and then stitch in all directions with lines crossing to make a new design. You could add little pieces of interfacing, paper, scraps of felt or leather, securing them with more lines of stitching. Lay massed thin threads on a piece of fabric and machine lines over them to hold them down. The threads will move slightly as you stitch, but this adds to the overall texture. Variegated and shaded threads are wonderful for this type of stitching. Whatever you try, once some of the machining is worked, sponge or spray colour on to parts of it. You may feel reluctant to do this is case you ruin the whole thing, but it adds so much interest by colouring both the fabric and the stitching. Now add more machined lines, remembering that much more stitching is required than you would think. To be really effective, these are not five-minute exercises, but you will find them very rewarding.

Appliqué

There are many books dealing with the intricacies of appliqué as a technique in its own right. Satin or zigzag stitches are often associated with machine appliqué, but combined with running stitch, appliqué offers great possibilities for a free approach. Nylon iron-on bonding agents such as Bondaweb, made by Vilene (Pellon), are an ideal way to secure the pieces to be applied to the background fabric. You can buy this in small packets or by the metre for larger projects, and instructions for its use are included. A word of warning if you are bonding sheer fabric to sheer fabric. Protect your ironing board with greaseproof paper, lifting the fabrics off the paper before they cool. Otherwise you may find that you have a sticky

5 *Strips of space-dyed thin silk were bonded to calico, then a flower cut from a printed cotton fabric was bonded on top. The applied pieces are secured with lines of straight stitching in varied colours.*

ironing board, as the bonding agent goes right through both layers of sheer fabric! Use simple shapes, adding lines or bands of stitching to secure the appliqué. Geometric shapes of different-coloured or textured fabrics look effective, some overlapped, and integrated with bands of machining. The bonding fabric does stiffen the fabric slightly, so bear this in mind when considering the purpose of the embroidery. For experimental samples, spray glue is quick and easy to use. For a softer effect, pin the pieces to be applied to the background fabric.

What to do with a failure

Every now and again, we all face the fact that the sample we are doing has gone wrong. It started with high expectations but has ended up dull or worse. The real problem is that although your confidence in the work is low, time has been spent, to say nothing of the fabric and thread used, and you feel reluctant to put it in the bin. You can remedy the situation, gaining enormous satisfaction from turning a disaster into a triumph.

7   *This fabric could be used to make a hat or a jacket.*

Solid stitching

Puckering, odd lines of stitching without purpose, with bumps of fabrics between may be the cause of the problem. Start with a small area, working solid dense stitching into the pucker, and you will find that it disappears.

Solid stitching is time-consuming to work, as you have to turn the fabric every time you come to the end of a line. Look in your manual to see whether you can reduce the foot pressure on your machine. If so, it will mean that you can move the fabric backwards and forwards under the presser foot while stitching, covering the ground much more quickly. You will also be able to work curved lines more easily.

Keep on stitching, changing directions, until whole areas are covered with machining. Miraculously, the more you stitch, the less it puckers.

Unite the whole

Perhaps you have used too many colours and certain parts look too garish. Do not try to unpick it -- this is virtually impossible with machine embroidery. Use one of the colours you like in the piece to stitch into all the other areas, not to cover them completely, but to tone them down and unite the various parts.

Cut it up

Our final solution may seem drastic, but we sometimes say to our students, 'cut it up and rearrange it'. It seems strange to take a pair of scissors to a piece of embroidery but, rearranged, it often looks much better. Stitch it all on to a new piece of fabric, machining over the cut edges, adding more stitching. An alternative is to cut the embroidery into strips, weave them together, and add lots of little tassels.

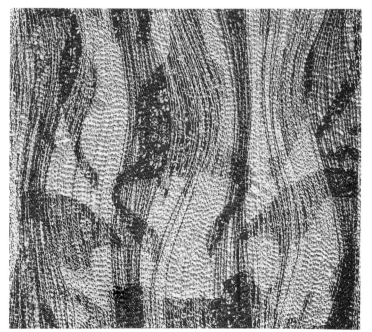

6   *An Art Nouveau shape cut from gold lamé was bonded to gold printed cotton. Massed wavy lines of running stitch in gold, silver and black secure and decorate the appliqué, and give a wonderful handle to the fabric. The massed stitching was necessary to reduce the puckering.*

Two threads in the needle

When the aim is to produce really solid stitching, it is helpful to have two threads in the needle. Obviously this will give denser stitches as well as the opportunity to mix colours as you work. Your machine may have two spool pins, or a hole for a second one to be positioned. If you have only one, check whether your bobbins will fit on the spool pin. If they will, wind a bobbin with one colour and place it on the pin with the second colour reel of thread on top of it. Perhaps you have only one spool pin and the bobbin does not fit on to it. There is always an answer. Place the second choice of thread in a little spice jar or bowl behind the machine, bringing the end of the thread up around the base of the spool pin. Whatever method you use, take both threads and pass through the threading system up to the tension disc. This may be horizontal or vertical, but either way, place one thread at each side of the disc so that both threads are under tension. Continue as normal threading the machine and the needle. Begin by using thin threads, change your

needle to size 100 and loosen the top tension slightly. Once you have tried this, you will see the possibilities of colour mixing and solid stitching in a new light.

9 *Drawing of a jacket to be made from this fabric, which is soft yet firm and drapes well.*
LINDA RAKSHIT.

8 *A similar fabric made by bonding scraps of rich metallic fabrics to calico, covered with massed stitching in metallic threads.*

Twin needles

Most modern machines will take twin or triple needles, giving you close parallel lines of stitching. Your dealer should have these in stock. They look rather strange, with two or three needles fitted into one shaft. Check your manual for instructions on threading, taking the opportunity to

Top tension	-- Normal to tight
Bobbin tension	-- Normal to tight
Presser foot	-- Grooved
Feed dog	-- Up
Stitch length	-- Any
Stitch width	-- 0 to narrow
Fabric	-- Unframed
Needle size	-- Twin or triple

use two or three different colours or variegated threads. The bobbin has one thread as usual. Pin-tucking feet are also available as an extra accessory, with three, five, seven or even nine grooves for use with twin needles. Work straight or curved lines, experimenting with altering the needle position to give broken lines of stitching. Increasing the tensions slightly, especially the lower one, will give a raised, pin-tucking effect. A fine Italian quilting can be achieved by turning the work over and threading a thicker yarn through on the reverse to raise the surface parallel lines.

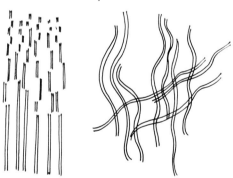

10 *Diagrams of patterns using twin-needle stitching. One with wavy lines crossing each other; another with straight disconnected lines achieved by altering the position of the needle.*

11 Left *A piece of fabric with twin-needle pin-tucks was cut into strips and re-applied to another fabric with extra stitching and narrow ribbons woven through.*

12 Right *Massed lines of twin-needle stitching were worked on a fabric sponged with coloured and gold fabric paint. The areas between the stitching were stuffed.*

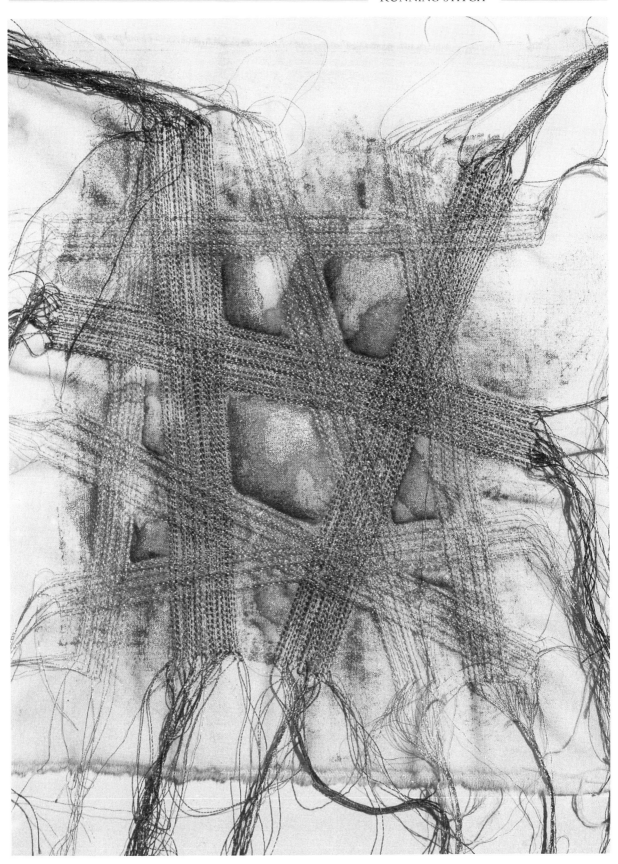

Stitch and slash

Many different types of fabric have been mentioned. Now consider sandwiches of two or three layers, making the combinations as interesting and varied as you can. Very surprising effects can be achieved by including fur fabric or wadding as part of the sandwich. Stitch through all the layers, working in parallel lines, making patterns of curves, squares or whatever you wish. Then, using sharp embroidery scissors, carefully cut away the top fabric between the lines of machining to expose the 'filling' underneath. For more complex variation, put even more layers of fabrics together, cutting down to different layers in various parts of the design. The weave and type of fabric used is important for this technique, so experiment with a wide variety to achieve the most exciting effects.

Top tension	-- Normal to tight
Bobbin tension	-- Normal
Presser foot	-- On or reduced pressure
Feed dog	-- Up
Stitch length	-- Any
Stitch width	-- 0
Fabric	-- 2 or more layers
Needle size	-- 90

Free running stitch

The two advantages of free running stitch are that you can stitch easily in any direction and that you can see exactly where you are going. Certain adjustments need to be made to your machine which may at first seem complicated, but which in no time at all will become second nature. For normal stitching, the fabric is held between the presser foot and the teeth or feed dog, and it is the action of

13 *Three layers of fabric – a backing, painted wadding and organza – were stitched together. The top layer was slashed to reveal the wadding.*
MARIAN MURPHY.

the feed dog which propels the fabric along under the needle. Free stitching requires the removal of these two functions to enable you to take control. On some machines the feed dog is lowered beneath the throat plate by a button or lever, so check in your manual to locate this. Other machines have a plate which fits over the feed dog, usually called a cover plate. The presser foot must be removed, including the short shank if your machine uses clip-on feet. Thread the machine with a good-quality cotton or synthetic thread, using a size 90 needle. Choose a cotton-type fabric and frame it, very tightly, in a ring frame. It cannot be stressed too much that the fabric must be *drum tight,* preferably in a wooden frame with both rings bound with tape to improve their grip. Set the stitch length to 0 as, from now on, the movement of the frame will determine the stitch length. Place the framed fabric under the needle. The bobbin thread should be brought up to the surface as it will otherwise get tangled underneath. Turn the flywheel towards you, dipping the needle into the fabric and back up to its highest position, which brings the bobbin thread up. Lower the presser foot lever, even though you have no foot in place, as this lever engages the upper thread tension system. Every machine embroiderer forgets to do this once in a while, as the lever is out of sight at the back of the machine. If you do forget, you will get a memorable tangle of loops.

If you are a beginner, this may seem a long list to remember but, with a little practice, it will take only a minute to change the machine over for free embroidery and back again for ordinary sewing.

Lower the needle into the fabric, hold the two threads, and begin stitching, running the machine at a medium speed. Move the frame steadily, enjoying the freedom of being able to stitch in any direction. Do try to relax, as the machine will sew happily wherever you move the frame. We once had a student who took

Top tension	-- Normal
Bobbin tension	-- Normal
Presser foot	-- Off
Feed dog	-- Lowered or covered
Stitch length	-- 0
Stitch width	-- 0
Fabric	-- Framed
Needle size	-- 90

a deep breath and held it while machining. This is not a good idea, especially if working on a large project. Give yourself plenty of time to practice, look at the diagrams and try to follow a pattern of lines as shown.

14 *Diagrams of simple stitching which will give a change of tone or colour.*

Starting and finishing a thread

Make a habit of holding the top and bobbin threads when you start to machine, and sew a few stitches on the spot to secure them. When you have stitched a short way, they can be snipped off close to the fabric. Finish in the same way, and you will find that the stitches do not unravel. There may be some practical items when you need to take both threads to the back of the fabric to be tied and cut. When you remove the frame from the machine, raise the presser foot lever and put your finger against the needle to support it. If you just pull the frame, the needle bends, which weakens it, causing eventual breakage.

Free running holding down fabric pieces

Your first attempts at free running stitch may look a bit haphazard. Make sure you are sitting comfortably, with your elbows supported and your hands relaxed holding the frame. It is a great help to have a purpose to your stitching, rather than aimlessly meandering around the frame. Choose some scraps of fabric, securing them to the background with an iron-on bonding fabric or spray glue. Don't worry about a design at this stage, as little squares, strips and rectangles work very well. Stitch over the fabric pieces in all directions. Imagine the needle is a pencil, shading in the background areas between the shapes with close lines of colour.

15, 16 *Two samples of pieces of silk secured to a ground fabric with massed lines of free running.* ROS ARNO.

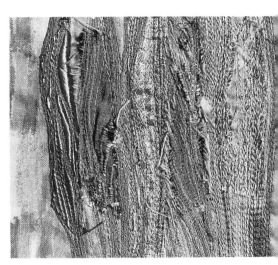

If you find that the top thread breaks while you are trying to master free running stitch, don't panic. Make sure that you are holding the frame down on the bed of the machine and moving it steadily, rather than in jerks and bursts. If the thread still breaks, refer to the 'Troubleshooting' section on page 140.

Patterns

Just as you would doodle with a pencil, making patterns, the same can be done on the machine. It is an excellent way of becoming familiar with the feel of the frame under the needle, as most of the patterns have a repetitive rhythmic quality. Try a shaded or variegated thread to see how areas of colour or changes of tone alter the pattern. Make some of them more dense by repeating the pattern again over the top. As you stitch, your imagination and the machine will invent many new doodles.

Tensions

You will discover that different movements of the frame alter the look of the stitch. In parts you may have a long stitch length, while in others you cannot distinguish one stitch from another. This depends on the speed of the machine in relation to how quickly or slowly you move the frame. You may also find that on tight circles and curves you see speckles or loops of the lower colour thread. Do not worry about this and think that your tension is 'wrong'. It adds interest and texture and becomes part of the pattern you are making. Try the same pattern first with the same colour on the spool and bobbin and secondly with a contrasting colour. Remember that you are embroidering, not making a skirt.

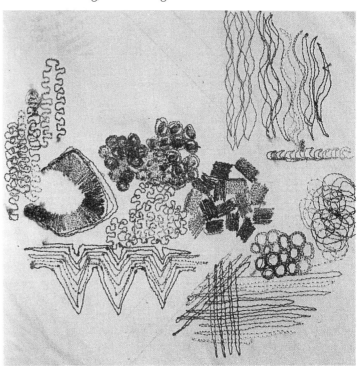

18 Above *Sample showing some of these patterns stitched.*

17 Left *Diagrams of some patterns using free running which can be used to fill areas in an embroidery.*

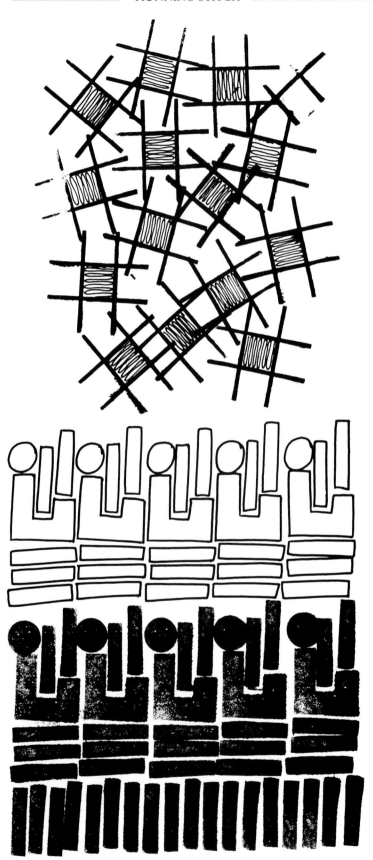

Gaining confidence

Planning and embroidering a design works wonders for your confidence. It gives purpose to your practice, setting up a chain of thinking of what you will make and how it will look. We mentioned in the Introduction the value of fabric printing to give you a starting point. Even if you have not had much experience, there are some very simple and quick ways of printing. Small jars of ready-to-use permanent fabric paint are available from Dylon in the UK. Put blobs of two or three colours on an old plate. Using a paint brush, lightly swirl the colours together but do not mix them completely. The colours blending together give a softer look than one strong colour on its own. Pre-wash and iron a piece of cotton fabric or calico and lay it on newspaper on a flat surface. You are now ready to print patterns directly on to the fabric with cut pieces of sponge, the edge of a piece of card, bottle tops or even the familiar potato. Whatever you use, touch it lightly in the fabric paint on the plate and then print on to the fabric. Have a spare piece of fabric nearby to try out each pattern. The colours are set by ironing with a hot iron when you have completed the design. Children's printing sets are marvellous, and much inspiration can be gained from children's television programmes. Work free running stitch to fill in shapes, as outlines or between the printed patterns. These simple ideas are often most effective and great fun to work.

19 Above *Printed lines made by using fabric paint on the edge of a piece of card, filling in the spaces with free running stitch.*

20 Below *A more complex pattern using outlines and fillings in free running stitch.*

Use of the darning foot

Confidence and control go hand-in-hand when working free running stitch. You might find that the use of a darning foot helps your confidence. The fabric can still be moved around freely and, providing it is firmly woven or backed with a stabilizer, a frame is not always necessary. (There are of course times when it is impossible to use a ring frame. Velvet fabrics wculd be marked by a frame, for instance, and where you are stitching very solidly on a large project, framing could sometimes be very difficult.)

Keep the feed dog lowered and frame the fabric, putting it under the needle before you fit the darning foot. Try free running stitch and decide whether you feel happier with the foot in place. It is not quite as easy to see where you are stitching, but there is a horseshoe-shaped darning foot available for some machines which is a great improvement. Then choose a firm fabric like felt or pelmet-weight interfacing, stitching with the darning foot on but no frame. You will have to hold the sides of the fabric instead of the frame to control the stitching. Each time you machine, decide which combination suits you and your purpose – framed and no foot, framed and the darning foot or unframed and the darning foot.

21 *Stitches of different lengths in free running using variegated threads. Rain suggested by threading pins through stitch loops.*
DELLA BARROW.

Quilting

English quilting is a sandwich of three layers – a backing, wadding and the top fabric, and it is a technique ideally suited to running stitch. The machined lines compress and sink into the fabric, showing up the unstitched areas in relief. A simple geometric design can be worked with the presser foot on and the feed dog up. Alternatively, reduced foot pressure gives you reasonable freedom to follow curved lines. A darning foot, with or without a frame, should be used when the design is intricate.

Prepare the three layers as you would for hand quilting, especially if you are going to use reduced foot pressure or a darning foot. Tack through the three layers, with both horizontal and vertical lines, to stop the layers moving against each other as you stitch. One or two layers of felt behind the top fabric give a slightly quilted effect, and are easy to handle. Quilting is not only a pattern of outlined shapes. It can be very effective used as dense stitching in the background areas or to fill the design itself. A typical feature of quilting is the contrast of heavily stitched areas with parts of the design left as plain, padded fabric.

22 *Design sprayed on to fabric using a stencil and then quilted with running stitch.* DEBORAH VAUGHAN.

Background areas

As soon as a design is placed within a shape – a circle, square, triangle or border – *negative* or *background* areas are created. These are often as interesting as the design itself. Practise on paper, seeing how many different patterns you can make to fill the background around a simple motif: contour lines following the silhouette, vertical, horizontal, diagonal or wavy lines, wiggly patterns or circles. You could try these patterns in running stitch using a shaded or variegated thread, or a metallic thread on a dark-coloured fabric, which would look very rich. The choice of fabric makes a difference to the effect,

so experiment with velvet, suede, felt, or on your own printed or space-dyed fabrics. All these suggestions for working the background areas would combine well with quilting designs.

23, 24 Top and above *Suggested patterns which use straight and contour lines in the background to show the motifs in relief.*

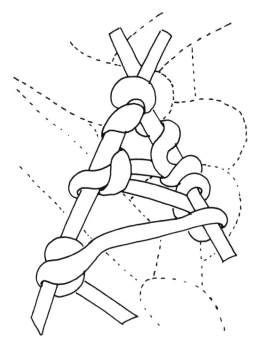

25 Above *A knot laid over an enlarged version of itself, drawn to indicate how the background area can be broken up.*
Various patterns or textures, or stitching in different directions, can be worked in the areas.

Variations on backgrounds

When the design is very intricate or delicate – a flower, perhaps – it makes even more sense to consider embroidering the background. Transfer the design on to the back of the fabric, working a fine line of free running stitch around the outlines. Turn the fabric over, reframing it. Use the outline as a guide for working a very dense pattern of free running stitch, right up to the line. Work until you cannot see a single speck of the background fabric. The close texture produced is very exciting and contrasts beautifully with the areas of plain fabric.

26 *Part of a quilted waistcoat in grey satin, with massed areas of stitching in shades of grey.* PADDY KILLER.

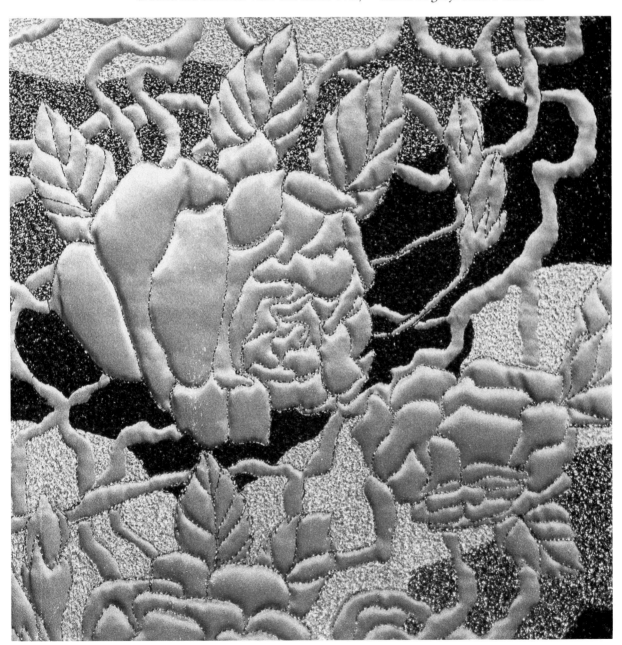

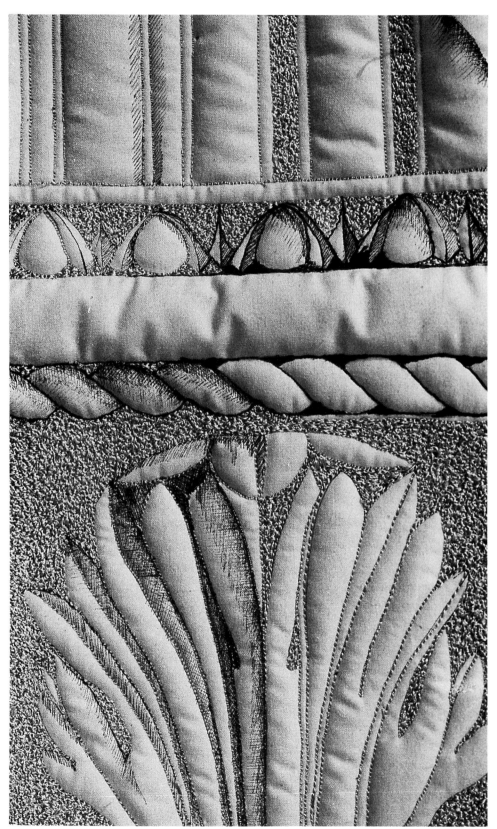

27, 28 *A sample of quilting with solid texture in the background to contrast with the plain fabric. Some shadow areas are drawn in with a fine pen. The diagram shows the movements used to build up this texture.*
PADDY KILLER.

Couching

It would require a great deal of control to stitch down a thick thread with free running stitch. A much freer couching can be worked, giving a lovely all-over textured pattern. Frame a piece of fabric and lay a textured slub yarn in swirls all over the surface. Work free running stitch in a meandering pattern to secure the textured yarn. You will need to use the darning foot for this technique, as otherwise the needle will lift the yarn away from the fabric. It tends to get pushed about by the darning foot as you stitch, but this can be controlled by easing it back under the foot with a stiletto. When the yarn is reasonably firmly secured, work massed free running stitch into the areas of background fabric which are still visible. Coloured or metallic variegated threads are particularly effective for this technique.

30 *Diagram showing a free couching pattern.*

29 *Bag with couched slub yarns and patterned metallic organza worked on to felt using variegated metallic thread. Pieces of solidly stitched fabrics secured to the surface, all worked in free running stitch.* PAMELA WATTS.

31 Right *Bag made by applying strips of silks and felt with burnt edges to a backing of felt, which had been baked in an oven until it was a golden caramel colour. The strips are secured with massed lines of free running stitch using a variegated metallic thread.* VALERIE CAMPBELL-HARDING.

32 Below *A textured slub yarn laid on calico, secured with free running stitch using the darning foot. Variegated metallic thread was used to fill in the background spaces between the slub yarn.*

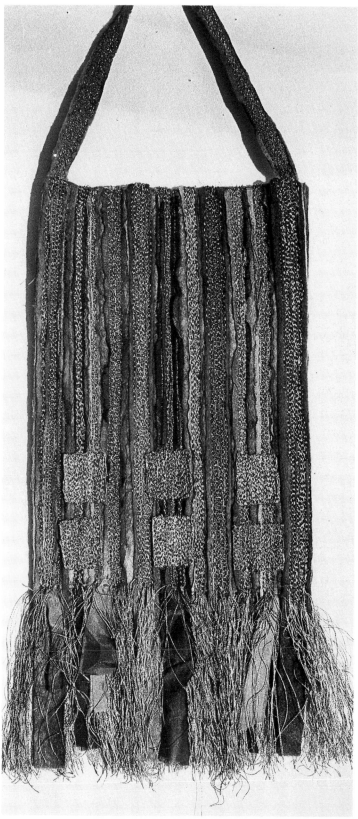

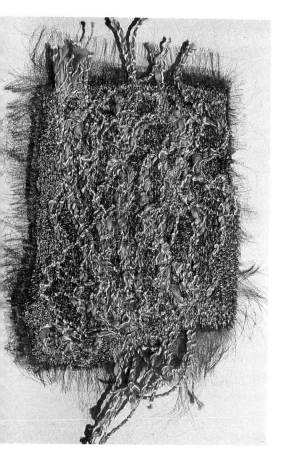

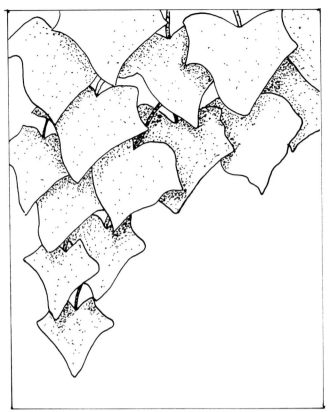

Water-soluble fabrics

One of the most exciting products to appear on the market in recent years is water-soluble fabric. There are two kinds: one fabric which looks and feels like organdie and another which is nearer to a plastic, rather like shower curtains. They both dissolve completely in water, the organdie type in boiling water and the plastic type in cold water. You can machine on them just as you would on ordinary fabric, although it is wise to practise before embarking on an ambitious scheme. When the work is placed in water, only the stitching will remain, so make sure that your machined lines are overlapped and connected in some way. This product definitely opens up new possibilities for machine embroidery.

33   Above left *Drawing of overlapping ivy leaves.*

34   *Design taken from the edges of ivy leaves.* MARGARET ROSS.

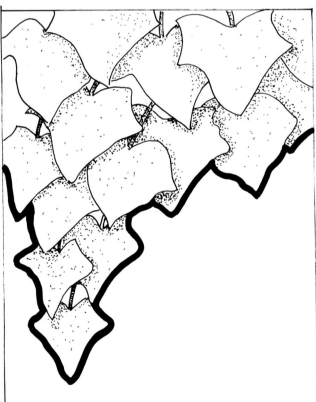

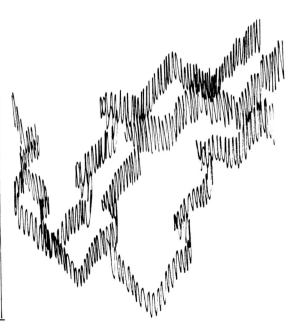

Edges

Many exciting effects can be planned using water-soluble fabrics to produce fringing on the edge of a fabric. Tack a piece of the soluble fabric to the edge of an ordinary fabric and frame with the join in the centre. (It might seem quicker to join the two with a line of machining but this would remain on the edge of the fabric, spoiling the effect of the fringe.) Work running stitch over both fabrics, crossing the join. Short lines of stitching on the soluble fabric give a frilly edge, while longer rows make a fringe. When the stitching is completed, cut away the excess soluble fabric up to the stitched areas. If you have used the plastic-type fabric, place the embroidery in a bowl of cold water. The organdie type should be placed in a flat dish before pouring a kettle of boiling water over it. The stitching will wrinkle up in an alarming manner, but it can be quite effective used like this. Alternatively it can be pinned out, flat and stretched, to dry. Heavy stitching in some areas may delay the dissolving of the fabric. This can give the interesting effect of a stiffened piece of stitching. However, a gentle simmer on the stove will remove every trace of the organdie-type soluble fabric, if this is what you require.

Making a fabric

Water-soluble fabric can play its part in the construction of a whole new fabric. This can combine some solid areas of fabric with areas of lacy stitching and is surprisingly strong and durable. You require some sort of grid pattern as a base. For this, choose ribbons, fabric rouleaux, strips of felt, braids or frayed strips of fabric, tacking them to a piece of water-soluble fabric. Make the grid of horizontal and vertical lines or a diagonal pattern. It can be regularly spaced or quite irregular. Use free running stitch to work across the areas of soluble fabric, stitching on to the fabric of the grid with each line. The machining can be delicate

35 *Layers of shot nylon organza were tacked on to hot-water-soluble fabric with free running stitch worked over the edges. These were mounted to hang in layers on a box construction. Two layers of stippled silk organza were bonded together and burnt into ivy leaf shapes, then attached to cover the top and sides of the box.*
MARGARET ROSS.

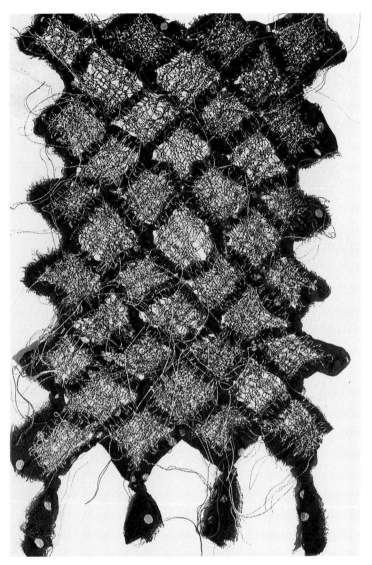

and open or very dense. A variation would be to alternate open and solidly stitched areas, or to work through a range of toning colours in the squares. When the water-soluble background has been dissolved away, your new fabric would make a most interesting part of a fashion garment.

Delicate fabrics

Your favourite supplier for embroidery materials will undoubtedly stock tempting nylon organzas, shot organdie and all manner of metallic and printed sheer fabrics. They can, of course, be used for appliqué or as frayed scraps to add texture and colour. If you want to use them alone as a background fabric, however, be prepared for a change in the appearance of your stitching. Fine lines of running stitch slightly pucker the surface, especially when working in circles or curves. You may find that the bobbin thread colour tends to come to the surface, even with normal tensions. Use these effects positively, exploiting the delicate nature of the fabrics. Try stitching patterns all over silk or nylon organza for a scarf, making the slightly gathered effect an integral part of the surface.

36   *A fabric made by tacking strips of torn fabrics to hot-water-soluble fabric in a grid pattern. The squares were filled in with free running stitch in two directions.* MARIAN MURPHY.

37   Opposite *Girl scarecrow constructed with stiffened torn calico. A pattern of leaves worked in free running stitch on silk organza falls from her shoulders.* GILL SMITH.

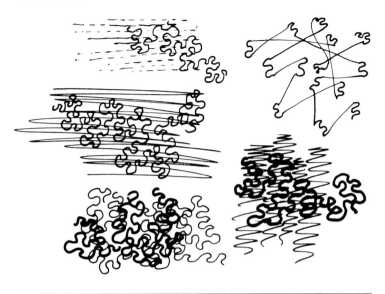

Vermicelli

This is a delightful pattern, a meandering line, which can be used for so many effects. You need to feel relaxed to work it successfully, as it has a flowing rhythm with no unplanned jerks or bursts of speed. Look at the diagrams of patterns, trying them out in a shaded or variegated thread. It is a useful technique for shading an area or adding subtle texture. Use nylon invisible thread on a dark fabric, or cream, shiny rayon on calico. Worked in layers, it is one of the best ways of increasing the tonal value of an area. It can also be used over other stitch techniques, as a filling for part of a design, or used to pattern the background area.

38 *Variations on the vermicelli pattern worked over free running stitch, zigzag, cable stitch and in disconnected bursts.*

39 *A sample of vermicelli worked in layers on net which was backed with water-soluble fabric.*

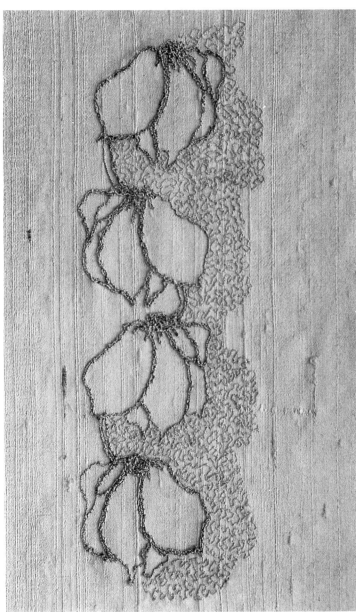

40 *Detail of vermicelli used as a background pattern to a simple design of fuchsias worked on fine silk.*

41 *Drawing of the blouse.*
LINDA RAKSHIT.

42   *Landscape worked in free running stitch using metallic threads on a background of painted calico.*
MARION BROOKES.

Landscapes

Looking carefully at paintings and drawings of landscapes provides many ideas on how free running stitch could be used to interpret them. It is the direction of the lines which is important, whether they are horizontal, angled or cross-hatched, or massed areas contrasted with empty peaceful areas. Start with just a simple sketch, a small area which appeals to you. Make a conscious effort to change the length of the stitch in different areas, by moving the frame more quickly. This will give a textured effect if built up in layers of stitching. Tighten the top tension to allow speckles of the bobbin thread to show on a stitched line. This can be very effective if the bobbin thread colour is changed often, to give shadows and areas of light across a landscape. Two threads in the needle provide the same effect, if you keep changing the colour of one of them. There is a temptation, especially if the stitching is going well, not to bother to change the top and bobbin threads. It only takes a moment, and a slightly different shade of a colour added to an area can make all the difference.

43   *Drawing of a landscape.*

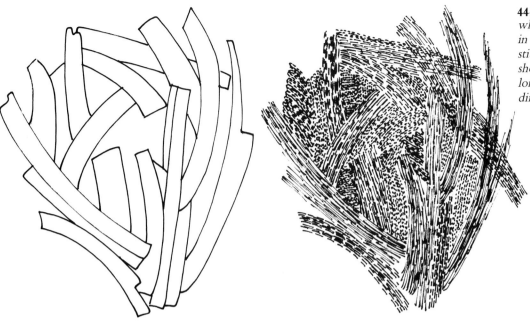

44, 45 *A pattern which can be filled in with free running stitch using very short, medium and long stitches to give different textures.*

46 *Silver and gold leathers were applied as a background to the coloured flowers, which were stitched with coloured threads in different directions. The leathers were stitched in silver and gold to break up the shine.* LINDA RAKSHIT.

Change of tone

One of the most exciting aspects of solid machining is the change of tone which occurs when there is a change of direction in the stitching. This is not really visible with single lines, but can be very marked if you work little squares of free running stitch in a basketweave pattern. Shiny rayon threads are particularly effective for this. This is one occasion when we recommend that you do *not* change the colour of your thread. Let the stitching change the colour for you.

Metal threads

The fine metallic threads made for machine embroidery are wonderful for directional changes in free running stitch. The play of light on the surface, combined with the rich sheen, makes the simplest embroidery look amazing. When using metallic threads, loosen the top tension. On most machines, they will break on normal tension settings, so reduce it, bit by bit, until the breaking stops.

47 *Patterns for solid stitching in different directions to give a change of tone.*

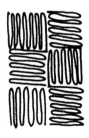

48 Top *Bag showing directional stitching using a variegated thread plus a coloured thread through the needle. The coloured thread was changed for every row. Black thread was used on the bobbin, with a slightly loose tension, allowing it to show on the edges of the squares. The tone of each square differs from the one next to it.*

50 *A bag made using a twist pattern, with copper and rust thread and copper and blue thread through the needle. The background uses copper and black thread.* VALERIE CAMPBELL-HARDING.

49 Left *Three patterns which make use of directional stitching to give a change of tone.*

2 Whip Stitch

This is a delightful stitch, more raised and textured than running stitch, and just as versatile. The top thread lies on the surface of the fabric and loops of the bobbin thread are brought up, through the fabric, to cover it. The normal stitches made by the top thread are not seen and the result is a corded, solid and yet flowing line. The adjustments needed to produce whip stitch vary slightly with every machine, but once mastered, it becomes a firm favourite. One of the main requirements for whip stitch is to run the machine fast and move the frame slowly and deliberately.

Select running stitch, remove the presser foot, lower the feed dog and frame the fabric. Choose two contrasting colour threads for the top and the bobbin, and make sure that the top thread is strong, either a good-quality cotton or one of the synthetic threads. Running the machine with normal tensions, you will see the top colour

Top tension	-- Tight
Bobbin tension	-- Normal or loose
Presser foot	-- Off
Feed dog	-- Lowered or covered
Stitch length	-- 0
Stitch width	-- 0
Fabric	-- Framed
Needle size	-- 90

51 *Whip stitch can be used as a line or a filling, and is very effective when every line is a different colour.*

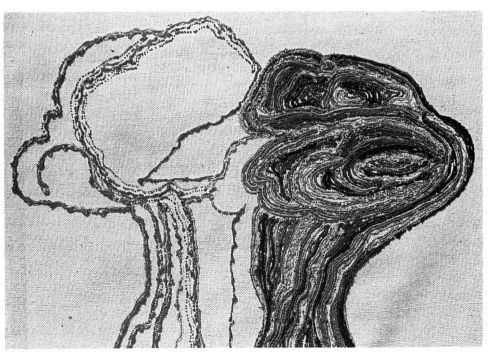

showing on the fabric. Slowly increase the top tension, bit by bit, until you see loops of the lower colour coming up to the surface. Now continue increasing the top tension until you have a solid line of the bobbin colour. If you touch this line of stitching with your finger, it will feel quite raised and textured. Under this tight top tension your top thread may snap. If this happens, the answer is to decrease the top tension a little, loosen the lower tension and the result will still be the same lovely whipped line. It is all a question of balancing the two tensions, and this balance is individual to every machine. Only very small tension adjustments will be necessary, so experiment until you are confident that the top thread will not break and the bobbin thread is whipping it. Using invisible nylon thread on the top produces instant whip stitch on some machines, so it is worth trying this. Another advantage of whip stitch is that you can wind the bobbin with the inexpensive rayon threads which tend to break easily, and the colour will show on the surface with little danger of their snapping.

53 *A sample of the stitched patterns using a shaded thread on the bobbin and transparent nylon thread through the needle.*

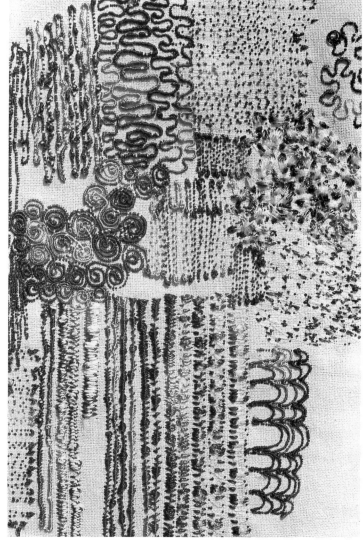

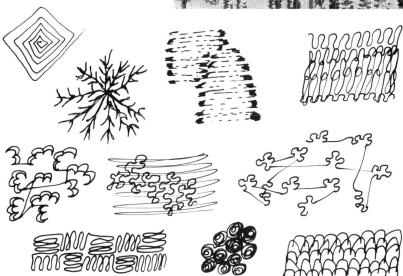

52 *Try some of these patterns to gain confidence with whip stitch.*

Gaining confidence

The following is a simple design which would be ideal as a practice exercise. It is much more satisfying to follow planned lines than to meander around a ring frame without any set purpose. Try this idea to increase your confidence with whip stitch, and think how it could be used as a border pattern for clothing or household items.

1 Lay a length of string on a piece of paper, making some interesting loops and twists. Make sure that the outside shape is not too regular. Draw all around the outside of the string with a fine black pen (fig. 54a).
2 On a piece of tracing paper, trace down one side only of the drawing, move the paper slightly and trace it

again. Then move the paper again and trace down the other side (fig. 54b).
3 Place a piece of fabric over the top and trace the design on to the fabric, using a hard pencil (2H). In order to see the design through the fabric, you may have to tape it and the fabric to a window pane.
4 Frame the fabric and set your machine for whip stitch. Work lines of whip stitch on the drawn lines and next to them, changing the colour on the bobbin for every row (fig. 54c).

This could be worked on a fabric which has been sponged, painted or printed with the same design, using a string block. Develop it by working the design in running stitch, then moving the design and working it in whip stitch (fig. 54d).

54 *Simple design excercise for whip stitch.*

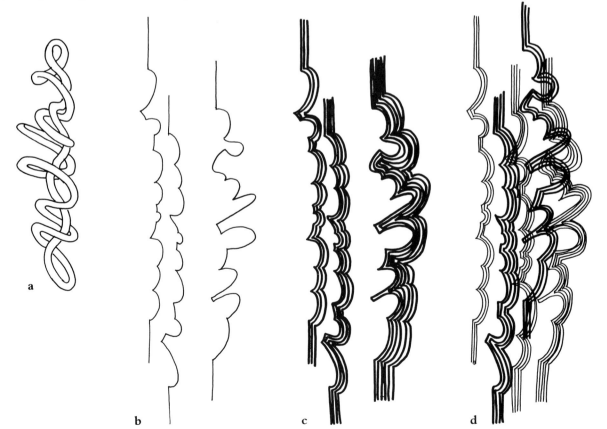

a

b

c

d

55 *Some patterns using whip stitch.*

a

b

56 *A bag stitched with square spirals using black, grey and white variegated thread in the bobbin and gold thread through the needle, on cream fabric. The edge was worked first in massed free running stitch. The tassels give movement to the design.* VALERIE CAMPBELL-HARDING.

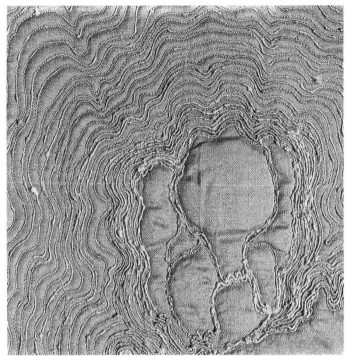

Background pattern

When a design or drawing has an interesting silhouette shape, consider filling the background area with contour lines of stitching. This is sometimes more effective than working out how to interpret the design itself. Take the opportunity of working in this way to experiment with a bolder colour scheme. Use different brightly coloured threads for each row or use one of the strongly contrasting variegated threads. An added bonus comes from the new shapes and patterns created and the integration of the design and the background. There are many alternative ways of patterning the negative areas. Try a meandering vermicelli, small circles or wavy vertical or horizontal lines.

57, 58 *Two designs in which the background is filled in with contour lines in whip stitch in different colours.*

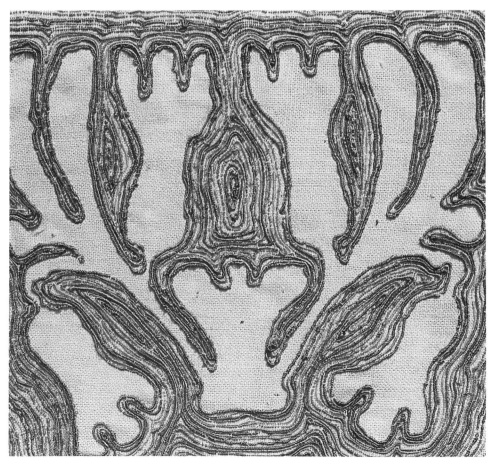

Solid and open patterns

The versatility of whip stitch is endless. It can be used as lines for the delicate tracery of leaves and flowers or built up into a massed area of pattern. One stitched line can look mean and uncertain, so, as in sketching, go over it with another line, then another, and a more confident and flowing style will result. Do not try to unpick a line – aim for rhythm, and any irregularities become part of the overall effect.

59 *To gain confidence with whip stitch, try working massed lines in this sort of pattern. Work it freely, without drawing on the fabric first.*

60 Right *Whip stitch flowers worked on a striped fabric.*

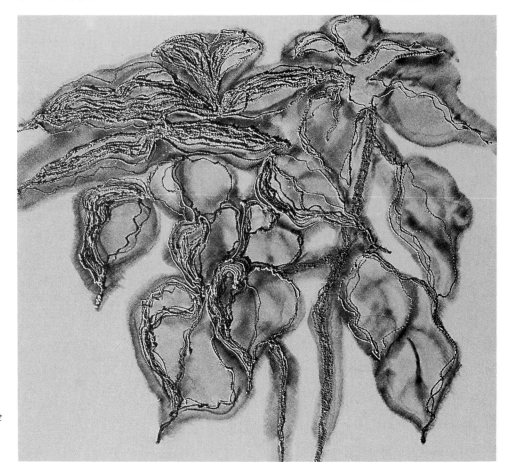

61 *Felt pen line drawing of poinsettias with colour wash on silk, and whip stitch using a variegated thread.* CELIA STANLEY.

62 *Landscape in whip stitch with felt pen lines added.*

63 *Log cabin patchwork bag made from strips of marbled fabric decorated with whip stitch before cutting.* KAY BALL.

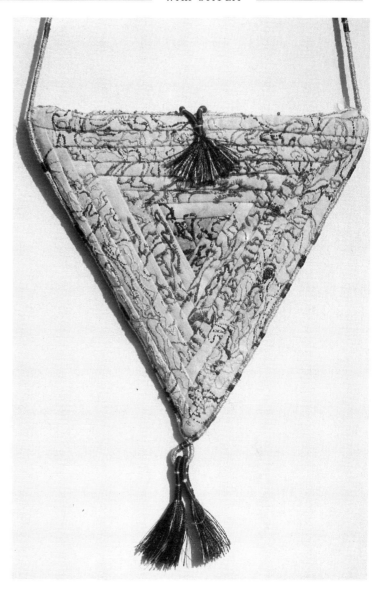

Patterned fabrics

Because the technique of working whip stitch is controlled and deliberate, it is an ideal stitch for enhancing patterned fabrics. The most exciting way of doing this is to pattern your own fabric with block or sponge printing, space-dyeing or marbling. Work lines of whip stitch into the colour areas and follow the swirls of pattern. With the popularity of printing and dyeing, most of us have a store of such fabrics, unused. One possibility is to machine on them, cut them into strips and use for one of the many patchwork methods. The bag shown in fig. 63 is made in a variation of log cabin patchwork and illustrates this technique perfectly. Whip stitch can be used as a pattern filling, worked in short lines in different directions. Fig. 62 inspires thoughts of transfer printing in the plain areas and mixing the colours in threads for the whip stitch areas. Do not discount bought patterned fabrics. Look at your own collection and see if any would benefit from lines of textured stitching before being cut into strips.

Whip stitch variations

The real fun of whip stitch comes with the subtle variations you can achieve. Contine to use contrasting colour threads for the top and the bobbin, so that you can see what is happening. Moving the frame more quickly will give a speckled line with more of the top thread showing; moving it very slowly will give a solid build-up of bobbin loops. This often happens when you change direction from forwards and backwards, as you instinctively slow down when turning a corner. Do this deliberately by stitching close lines in a band pattern and letting the bobbin colour build up at both edges. The variegated rayon threads are lovely in the bobbin, particularly with a metal thread on the top giving a glint to the surface of the work. (You will have to alter the balance of the tensions for this, reducing both of them to prevent the top metal thread snapping.) Experiment with nylon invisible thread for whip stitch, as this gives a frosted effect, almost like icicles. As your confidence grows, you will learn to control exactly where and how the bobbin colour appears by the speed of the machine and the way you move the frame. Work in deliberate jerks and pauses and try machining from side to side, as this will alter the appearance of the stitch. It can be everything from smooth and firm to irregular and mottled, just as you wish.

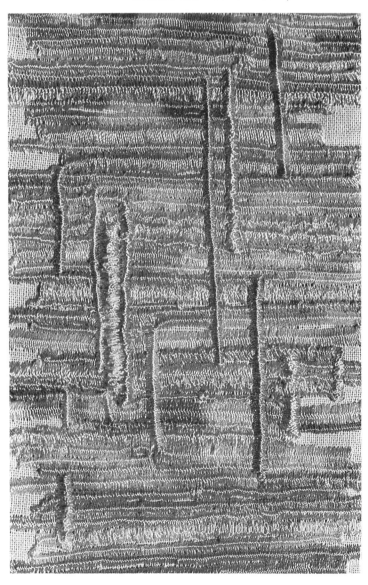

64   *Lines of satin whip stitch using coloured and variegated threads.*

65   *A pattern which could combine straight whip stitch in layers, and satin whip stitch giving a focal point.*

Whipped satin stitch

Satin as whip stitch gives a much thicker textured line and is a delightful combination of the two stitches. Set your machine for satin stitch, frame the fabric and thread the machine with different colours on the top and the bobbin. The tensions are basically the same as for whip stitch, with a tight top tension, but you will need to loosen the lower tension even more, or bypass it. As you stitch, moving the frame slowly, the colour from the bobbin comes up through the fabric in loops at both sides of the line and meets in the middle. This gives a more raised and textured line than ordinary satin stitch, and a much wider line than whip stitch.

66 *A photocopy of a landscape design using torn rubbings. The central strip was replaced with machine embroidery using variations of whip stitch and free running stitch.* LINDA RAKSHIT.

Combining textures

The texture of whip stitch is particularly attractive when worked in massed lines or areas of stitching. This quality is seen to great advantage when contrasted with some plain or smooth areas. Choose a drawing or design, pencil in the outlines and shade some areas to be filled in. Place the drawing behind the fabric and transfer the lines with a hard pencil. Work whip stitch for the outlines and close lines of whip in different directions for the solid areas. The plain parts could also be coloured with transfer dyes or fabric paints. This would be effective developed as a border pattern or as part of a larger design. Wrapping would combine well with whip stitch. Wrap strips of pelmet-weight interfacing or thin card by hand with threads of your choice. Secure to the background fabric with a few stitches, and work whip all around, making a dense area of contrasting textures.

67 *Whip stitch used as a contrast to long straight stitches worked by hand over padding. The design used folded strips of paper on a painted background. The pattern and texture of the paint suggested the flowing lines of stitching.* LINDA RAKSHIT.

Automatic patterns

Do try the automatic patterns on your machine with whip stitch settings. Some of them are more effective than others, but there will certainly be surprises in store. The straight stitch parts will be whipped with the bobbin colour, whereas the zigzag parts will be the top colour. Experiment with stitch lengths and stitch widths. You can, of course, work the automatic patterns as free stitching to increase the whip effect. This is not very satisfactory where part of the pattern is in reverse, as this action would normally be controlled by the feed dog.

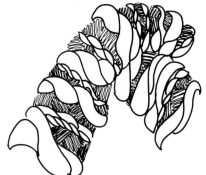

68   Above *A pattern which contrasts stitching with plain areas of fabric. This could be repeated to make a border pattern.*

Moss stitch

This is a further variation of whip stitch and relies on the same tight top tension and a very loose lower tension. It gives actual loops on the surface, more pronounced than the whipping or covering of the top thread. It is probably easiest to do on machines where you can bypass the lower tension system altogether. This is explained more fully in chapter 3 on cable stitch. An interesting effect is produced by working moss stitch and then withdrawing the top thread, leaving the loops. This can be done while the embroidery is still in the frame. You must either back the fabric with iron-on Vilene or apply glue to prevent the loops from unravelling.

Top tension	-- Tight
Bobbin tension	-- Very loose
Presser foot	-- Off
Feed dog	-- Lowered or covered
Stitch length	-- 0
Stitch width	-- 0
Fabric	-- Framed
Needle size	-- 90

69 *Moss stitch over pieces of transparent fabrics and ribbons.*

70 Below *An Art Nouveau pattern carried out in whip stitch and lines of loops.* THEA DE KOCK.

Feather stitch

At first glance this technique looks like a zigzag stitch, but it is produced by straight stitching worked in a tight circular pattern. The tension settings are the same as for moss stitch, with a very tight top tension and a very loose or bypassed lower tension. Do make sure that the top thread is strong and frame the fabric as tightly as you can, as there is considerable strain on both. As you stitch, the top thread is pulled into a tight circle and the bobbin thread comes to the surface in a spiky star pattern. This is very attractive worked in mass textured areas, stitching round and round in circles of different sizes. You will discover whether you prefer to work in clockwise or anticlockwise circles, and do try working lines in an 'S-bend' pattern. This can look untidy with just one line, so work many lines together for maximum impact.

Top tension	-- Tight
Bobbin tension	-- Very loose or bypassed
Presser foot	-- Off
Feed dog	-- Lowered or covered
Stitch length	-- 0
Stitch width	-- 0
Fabric	-- Framed
Needle size	-- 100

71 *Detail of a landscape combining whip and feather stitches.*

72 Right, above *Certain movements and patterns show feather stitch to advantage by bringing up long loops of the bobbin thread. These can be open and delicate, or massed and rich.*

73 Below *Feather stitch patterns using a variegated thread.*

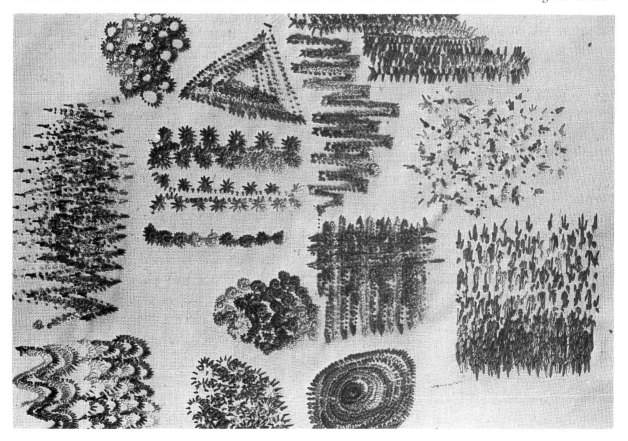

3 Cable Stitch

74 *A band of cable stitch using dishcloth cotton in straight, zigzag and automatic patterns, changing the stitch lengths. The second band of cable stitch uses a wide variety of threads, all with a very loose bobbin tension.*

Threads which are too thick to pass through the upper tension system and the needle can be wound on the bobbin; the underside of the work then becomes the right side. It is usually necessary to loosen the lower tension to allow the thick threads to pass through easily. These two factors – not being able to see what is happening as you sew and having to loosen the lower tension – sometimes deter machine embroiderers from working cable stitch. This is a pity, as it is really an easy and versatile technique.

Top tension	-- Normal
Bobbin tension	-- Loose
Presser foot	-- On
Feed dog	-- Up
Stitch length	-- Any
Stitch width	-- 0
Fabric	-- Unframed
Needle size	-- 90

Lower tension systems

Every machine seems to have a slightly different bobbin mechanism, so start by finding out how your lower tension system works. Some manuals give very little instruction, and if in doubt you should ask your dealer to explain more fully. There are two main types of bobbin system and both have a small screw which adjusts the degree of tension on the lower thread. If your bobbin is horizontal in the machine, there will be a small screw on the bobbin case which fits permanently in the machine. On machines where the bobbin is vertical, it will fit into a removable bobbin case and the screw is on the side of this. With the latter type of mechanism it is quite possible to loosen the screw completely, when it will surely fall to the floor and you will spend the next hour on your hands and knees searching for it. Always hold the bobbin case over a box lid or piece of fabric when making adjustments, or better still, get a spare screw and even a spare bobbin case, keeping the other

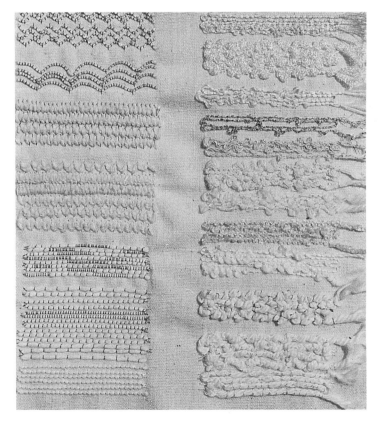

for ordinary sewing. Whichever system your machine has, draw yourself a little diagram in your manual showing exactly how the slot in the screw head is positioned, so that you can return the tension to normal at any time. Before you alter the lower tension do test normal tension by pulling on the thread and feeling the degree of resistance. Turning the screw in a clockwise direction increases the tension and turning anticlockwise decreases the tension. Sometimes only tiny adjustments of the screw are necessary, and even 5 or 10 'minutes' of a clock-face will alter the tension noticeably. At other times you may need 30 or 45 'minutes', and on occasions, no tension at all. On machines which have a horizontal bobbin case, turn the screw in an anticlockwise direction as far as it will go to loosen the tension completely. Don't worry as this type of screw will not fall out. Some machines of the horizontal bobbin type have a hole in the side of the bobbin case and you can pass a thick thread through this hole with the aid of a stiletto to bypass the tension. This is convenient, as then you do not have to adjust the screw at all. Where you have a removable case, turn the screw anticlockwise until it comes out and thread your thick yarn through the resulting hole. Make a note to remind you where you put the screw.

Stitching

Thread the top of the machine with a contrasting colour and normal tension. Place the fabric in the machine and bring the lower, thick, thread to the surface to prevent it becoming tangled underneath, as this is the *right* side of the embroidery. (You will have to pull on both sides of the loop of top thread and maybe pierce a hole in the fabric with a stiletto.) Run the machine at medium speed. You will have a line of normal stitching on the top and the thick thread will be couched underneath. If the top tension is slightly tight, the soft thread underneath will look

like beading. With a looser top tension the couched thread will be completely flat and smooth. Alter the stitch length to produce different results. A very short stitch length will give an effect like whip stitch, with the top thread almost totally encasing the lower thread.

Threads

Take time to practise with different threads in the bobbin, as an amazing variety can be used. On most machines it seems that it is the degree of softness of the thread that matters most. You will see on the sample in fig. 74 that we have used dishcloth cotton, chenille, 4-ply wool, lurex threads and bobbly knitting yarn. However, if your machine makes the slightest noise of protest, stop using

75 *Cable stitch worked with the foot on, combined with free running stitch. All the stitching was then painted with gold fabric paint, and more cable stitch added, using a thick Jap gold in the bobbin.*

that thread immediately, as every machine does have its limits. As well as thick yarns, wind many strands of thin threads together. The sample in fig. 74 used 12 strands of Rayon 40, but you could try multiple thin metal threads or mixed coloured and metallic threads. When hand-winding many thin threads together, do take care to wind evenly and smoothly, as it is quite easy to get into a tangle. Jap gold, used for hand metal thread embroidery, works very well, and rayon knitting ribbon yarn gives a really thick and textured effect.

76 *Cushion using massed running stitch on ribbons which were then applied to a fabric in a woven pattern. Cable stitch was added to blend the tones and colours.*
VALERIE CAMPBELL-HARDING.

Zigzag and automatic patterns

Set your machine for zigzag and experiment with different threads, stitch lengths and widths. If you use a contrasting-coloured thread on the top, this colour will show at each side of the line of zigzag. You may need to loosen the top tension a little and should certainly do so if using a metallic thread on top. The automatic pattern stitches work well, too, and could be a very practical addition for fashion garments. Do try a tight band of automatic patterns and not just one single line.

Hand-winding the bobbin

Choose a thread like soft embroidery cotton or cotton perlé 5 and hold the end of the thread against the rim of the bobbin with your thumb, or thread it through the slit or hole inside the bobbin. Wind a few times to secure the thread and snip off the loose end to prevent it catching on the tension spring. Continue winding the bobbin with a reasonable tension, but resist the temptation to fill it completely. Place the bobbin in the machine or the bobbin case and loosen the tension until the thread runs freely when pulled.

Stitching across space

In the sample in fig. 77 small squares of pelmet Vilene were stitched with a normal thread on the top and one strand of cotton perlé on the bobbin. Try machining across the square, over the edge and continuing stitching for approximately 7 to 10 cm (3 to 4 in.), pulling the square away from you at the back of the machine and sewing on nothing. Then continue stitching on to and across the next square. This technique is explained more fully in chapter 6.

77 *Multi-coloured cable stitching worked across pieces of pelmet interfacing and the spaces between them. The pieces were twisted so that the loose threads wrapped around each other. They were then applied to a ground decorated with running stitch.*

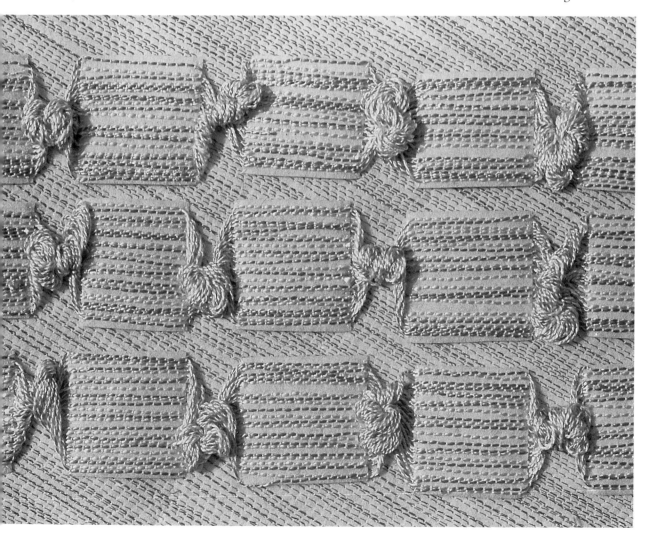

Free cable stitch

With the foot removed and the feed dog lowered, stitching in any direction is possible. Frame the fabric and choose a good-natured soft thread for the bobbin. If you loosen the lower tension completely or bypass it, a lovely textured line will be made. Don't forget to bring the lower thread to the surface, and work in close areas of stitching, imagining the foliage of bushes, bark or mosses. Under these conditions most machines will give a really textured stitch, but moving the frame slowly, making short stitches, seems to accentuate this. Sometimes a very narrow zigzag (setting $\frac{1}{2}$ or 1) throws the lower thread from side to side and makes a more bobbled line. Do practise with as many threads as you can find: even with exactly the same tensions, different threads do give entirely different results. Some of our machines seem to love the rayon ribbon yarn for free cable stitch, and it produces an effect unlike any other stitch technique. The yarn could be space-dyed prior to use or have fabric dye sponged into the area after stitching. A thin soft chenille is equally spectacular, and the slub knitting yarns which have a thick bobble every two or three inches give areas of thin thread with patches of texture. The thread on the top of the machine gives variety, too.

Top tension	-- Normal
Bobbin tension	-- Very loose
Presser foot	-- Off
Feed dog	-- Lowered or covered
Stitch length	-- 0
Stitch width	-- 0
Fabric	-- Framed
Needle size	-- 90

78 *Free cable stitch used as textured lines to contrast with free running stitch. A very loose bobbin tension gives this effect.*

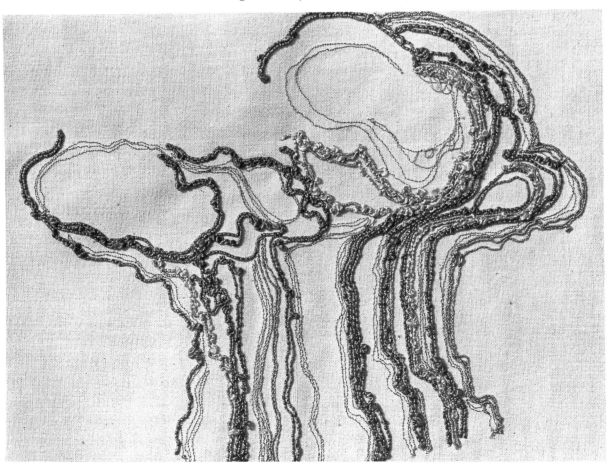

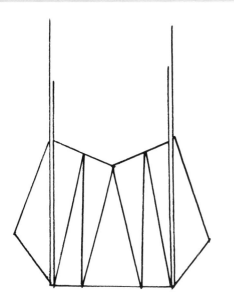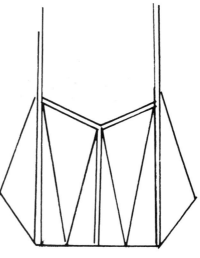

79 *Patterns for bags, which could have areas of massed cable stitch contrasting with plain fabric or smooth stitching.*

80 *Cushion with bands of cable stitch using many thin variegated threads together in the bobbin. The diagonal bands of cable had four strands of fine wool and rayon floss thread with a bypassed lower tension.* PAMELA WATTS.

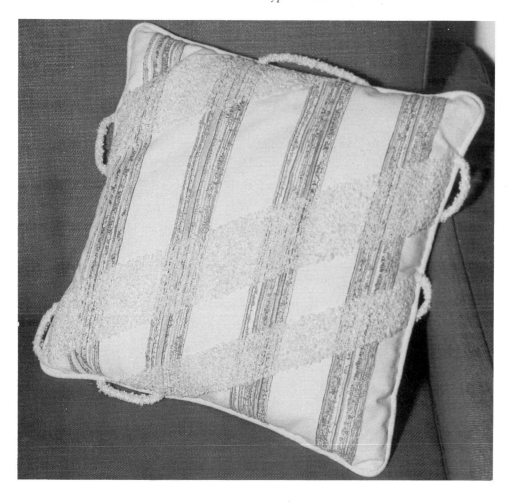

81 *Bag using space-dyed fine ribbon yarn in the bobbin with a bypassed lower tension. The bands of running stitch give a contrast of texture, worked with a bronze metallic thread on the spool and a bright pink on the bobbin showing through.* PAMELA WATTS.

A contrasting colour will speckle the lower thread colour, while a variegated colour on top will give tonal changes in the areas of texture below. If you are planning large areas of cable stitch do wind as many bobbins as you can before you start, as the thick thread runs out quickly.

When you have worked through the suggestions given for cable and free cable stitch, some of your uncertainties about this technique should disappear. There are positive advantages – the design can be drawn on the top of the fabric in the knowledge that this is, in fact, the underneath, and an area of texture can be stitched more quickly than with whip stitch, for example. Once you have chosen and practised with a fabric, top thread and bobbin thread, and decided on the tensions, your machine will continue to produce exactly the same texture, so the fact that you cannot actually see what is happening does not matter. This is a technique which combines well with contrasting areas of free running, whip or satin stitch. When an area of cable has been worked, take the fabric out of the frame, turn it over and reframe it; you can then work free running stitch to integrate the cable with the fabric. Stitch into the texture in areas to flatten it and change the colour tone.

82 *Squares and rectangles of cable stitch using a slub yarn with a background of free running stitch worked in different directions.*

Narrow bands

Strips of firm fabric or felt can be freely cable stitched, working right up to and over the edges. If you use a soft thread in the bobbin, you can turn the strip over and reverse the process so that both sides of the band are richly textured. These can be applied on to a fabric twisted or knotted, and would make interesting bag handles, belts or bracelets. You will need to use the darning foot for working on narrow strips, or stretch them tightly across a ring frame.

83 *Strips of felt were covered with cable stitch using a textured metallic thread. These were loosely plaited and applied to a background, densely worked in cable stitch using the same metallic thread.*

4 Zigzag Stitch

Most modern machines are swing needle machines which enable the needle to stitch from side to side, giving a zigzag stitch. While this is often thought of as a practical stitch in dressmaking or for simple appliqué, it offers enormous possibilities for building up areas of pattern, texture and colour blending for embroidery.

Top tension	-- Normal
Bobbin tension	-- Normal
Presser foot	-- Satin stitch foot
Feed dog	-- Up
Stitch length	-- Any
Stitch width	-- Narrow to wide
Fabric	-- Unframed
Needle size	-- 90

Setting up your machine

Your machine will probably have a lever or button to set the machine for sideways stitching and another lever or button for altering the width of the stitch. The stitch length control operates as normal, giving a wide-open zigzag on a long stitch length and close satin stitch on the shortest stitch length. Set up your machine with the zigzag foot, the feed dog up and normal tensions, and practise stitching lines of zigzag, altering the stitch width and stitch length as you sew. Work rows on top of each other to build up dense areas of stitching. If you use a variegated thread, a mottled colour effect will result instead of the distinct areas of colour seen in one line of stitching. Start stitching with the stitch width set at '0' and increase the width gradually as you stitch to obtain a tapered line, and finish by reversing the process. This can be more effective than starting with a wide zigzag. Interesting colour effects can be obtained by using two threads together through the needle, threading them one to each side of the tension disc. This is often effective when using two spools of

84 *Zigzag sample using stitching in one and two layers with satin stitch blobs for emphasis.*

the same variegated thread. Wind a bobbin with the thread and place it on the spool pin with the spool on top. Using a larger needle, try thicker top stitching threads and experiment with metal and invisible nylon threads.

Tensions

Generally, a slightly looser top tension is required for zigzag, and you should always reduce the tension when using metal threads. Although the top and lower tensions should be perfectly balanced for practical sewing, an interesting effect is achieved for embroidery if small loops of the bobbin thread are seen at the sides of the zigzag. Put a contrasting colour on the bobbin and increase the top tension very slightly; blobs of different colour will edge each line of stitching. If you are using a fine material zigzag tends to pucker it, so use two layers of fabric together or back the fabric with paper or tear-away backing.

Free zigzag

A wider variety of effects is possible with the feed dog lowered and the foot removed. Set the machine for zigzag, frame the fabric and select a stitch width. This mechanism still determines how far the needle travels from side to side, but set the stitch length at '0', as the way you move the frame will decide the openness of the zigzag. As well as stitching forwards and backwards, you can now move the frame from side to side, and this will give straight or curved lines of long stitches. This is effective using a shiny or metal thread, as the longer stitches catch the light and areas of stitching in different directions will give tonal changes of colour. Moving the frame at different speeds will allow a build-up of dense stitches in places and an open spiky effect in others. Practise building up these different textures, using the diagram of stitch patterns as a starting point. You will discover many more patterns of your own as you stitch.

85 *Sample of variations of zigzag stitching worked in layers, scallop pattern, over pieces of fabric and circles.*

Couching

Zigzag is a good technique for couching and for holding down a variety of items on a background fabric – not just thick threads, but cords, string, metal threads, strips of fabric, etc. If a simple or geometric design is planned, leave the presser foot on and the feed dog raised. Choose one of the many textured slub yarns and a stitch width which will allow the needle to go over the thread from side to side rather than through it. Check this by turning the fly wheel towards you, lowering the needle into the fabric at each side of the thick thread. Stitching over thick threads with zigzag will flatten the thread somewhat, but this can be an interesting change on chenille, for example. Do try close parallel lines of

Top tension	-- Normal
Bobbin tension	-- Normal
Presser foot	-- Off
Feed dog	-- Lowered or covered
Stitch length	-- 0
Stitch width	-- Narrow to wide
Fabric	-- Framed
Needle size	-- 90

86 *Tree of life chasuble. Detail of the trunk of an olive tree, in organza laid over pelmet interfacing. Assorted braids, cords, knitting yarns and threads laid with machine zigzag, using different tones of metallic copper and gold machine threads. It is handled very much as a tonal drawing on a natural silk tweed background. Designed and made by* JANE LEMON. *St Thomas' Church, Lymington.*

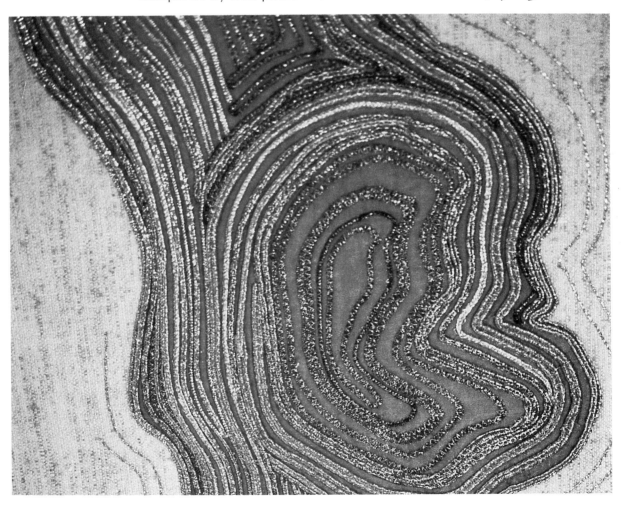

couched threads as a dense textured area of pattern, rather than a single line. Use firm string, a bundle of thin threads, Jap gold or lurex cords, a thin strip of fabric loosely twisted or frayed, thin ribbons, strips of metallic paper, thin acrylic rods or scraps of patterned or metallic fabrics. Your own store cupboard will provide endless inspiration.

Free zigzag for couching

With the presser foot removed and the feed dog lowered, a freer couching can be worked. Frame the fabric and pin, bond, glue or tack the scraps of fabric or thick threads in position, then zigzag both to hold them and to integrate them with the background fabric. The thread colour can match either the applied pieces or the background fabric. As a general principle, much more stitching is required than you would think. When you have finished, do still more stitching to build up dense areas of texture.

Zigzag for backgrounds

Pattern or shade the *background* of your design. This can be very subtle, using invisible nylon thread or a shiny cream rayon thread on calico. Sometimes, when a design looks a little stark, patterning the background with free zigzag lines can help to integrate the design with the fabric. When this technique is used on net or sheer fabrics, a lovely lacy effect is produced. Experiment with different colours on the bobbin, as this will show through to the right side.

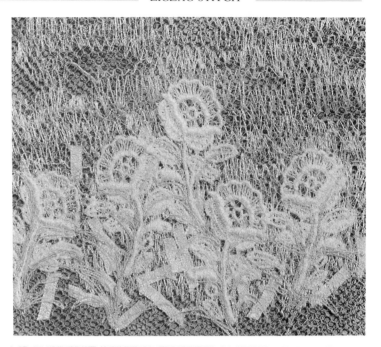

87 Above *Zigzag used as a background to lace flowers, built up with whip stitch.*

88 Right *Zigzag used as a background to applied shapes.* LINDA RAKSHIT.

Fabric manipulation

Many of these techniques can include zigzag stitching, either before or after the manipulation. Evenly spaced lines or grids of zigzag can actually make pleating and tucking easier. Mark lines on the fabric with chalk or water-soluble pen and stitch over with zigzag before removing the guide lines with a damp cloth. Use the grid as a basis for pleats, tucks or honeycomb smocking. An irregular pattern of criss-cross lines would make an interesting starting point for gathered quilting (puff patchwork) or could be cut into strips and used for log cabin patchwork.

Alternatively, prepare the fabric with pleats, tucks, folds, etc. and zigzag freely to hold or distort the fabric and add further decoration. Striped and geometric-patterned fabrics offer lots of ideas for experimentation.

89 Below *Pleated and piped silk which was previously decorated with lines of zigzag stitching to add colour and pattern.*

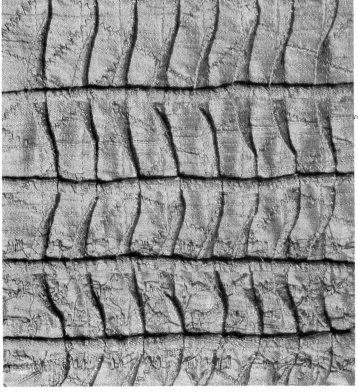

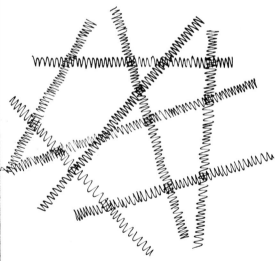

90 Above *Suggestions for zigzag patterns to decorate fabrics.*

91 Right *Samples of zigzag stitching on painted graph paper. Holes were torn in some places.* ALISON ELLIOTT.

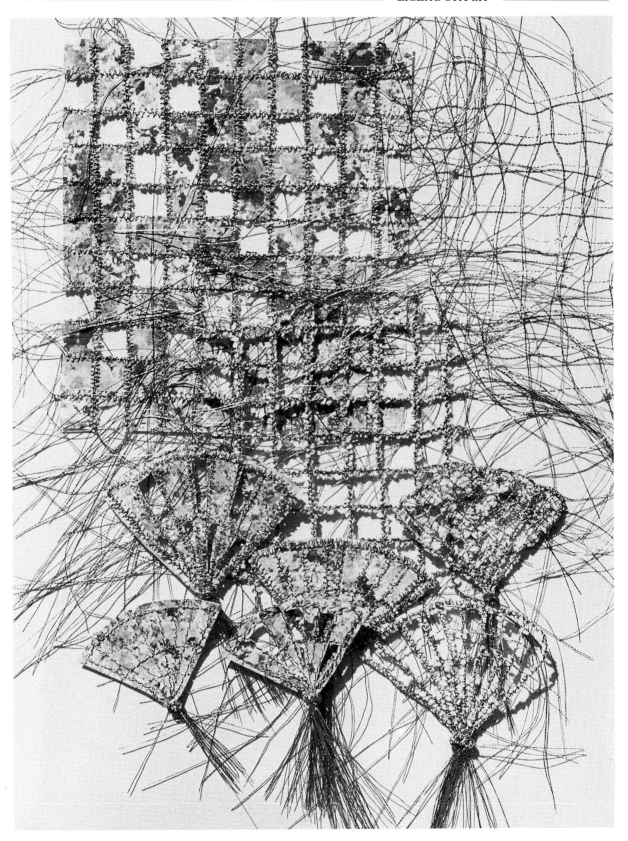

92 *Hanging c.35 in. × 39 in.*
(90 cm. × 100 cm). Printed background
covered, in parts, with organdie. Tonal
areas built up with scraps of nets, scrim
and calico secured with free running and
zigzag. JULIA CLOUGH.

Building up richness

Most embroiderers collect and hoard scraps of lurex fabrics and ribbons, lace, shot silks and organzas, and these can be built up into a really rich texture to make evening bags, belts and jewellery. Cut oddments of fabric, plait, twist or knot strips of fabric and threads, and zigzag freely using one of the multi-coloured metal threads. Again, when you think you have finished, keep on stitching until the whole area is totally integrated, rich and solid.

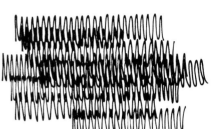

93 *Two diagrams showing zigzag stitching worked in layers to give richness.*

94 *Some machines have a very wide zigzag and the width can be varied as you stitch. Some parts of this embroidery have* one layer of stitching, some two or three layers. Knots of ribbon are added to give extra colour and texture.

Wrapping threads and string

Remove the presser foot, lower the feed dog and set the machine to a wide zigzag. Many kinds of string, cord or yarn can be wrapped, and the stitching can be close, covering the string completely, or more open. As well as stitching over one length of string or thread, you can make your own textured yarns. Choose four to six different threads such as mohair, slub yarns, and chenille, and include one smooth thread like soft embroidery cotton. Hold the bundle of threads tightly together in front of the needle and behind it, and don't forget to lower the presser foot lever. When you start to stitch, the spool and bobbin threads may disappear into the race and jam, so hold these threads together with the textured yarns for the first few stitches. When a length has been stitched, pull the smooth thread up and you will get a really textured and bobbly yarn which would be ideal for an interpretation of bark or

95 *Necklaces. Continuous lengths of string were machine-wrapped in coloured and metallic threads. Occasionally, tufts of thread were included in the wrapping.* VALERIE CAMPBELL-HARDING.

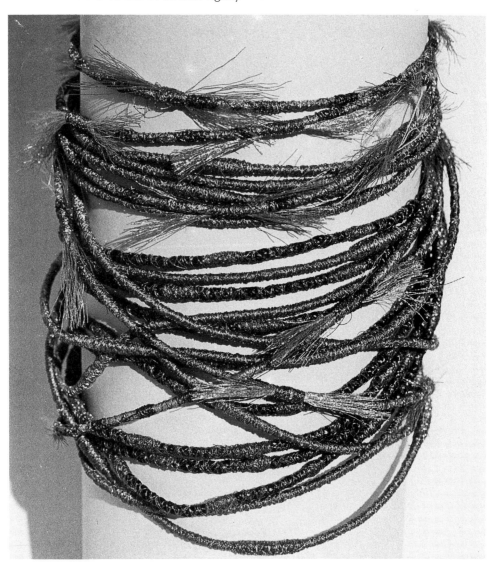

96 *A collar made from wrapped yarns joined to make a stretchy mesh fabric in reds and gold.* MARIAN MURPHY.

lichen. A wide-apart zigzag will encourage the threads to bubble out through the stitching, whereas a closer zigzag will give a much firmer yarn. Six strands or more of fine metallic thread stitched with the same metal thread could give many ideas for jewellery. To make the wrapping of threads much easier, purchase a single-hole cording foot as an extra attachment. Using this, you should leave the feed dog up and keep a fairly short stitch length.

Shell thread

Cut a 2–3 cm (1 in.) wide strip from tights (pantyhose) or a stretchy fabric, and pull it hard. Using the satin stitch foot with the feed dog up, place the strip under the presser foot to secure it and pull the fabric up between the toes of the foot at an angle to the needle. Set the stitch width to the widest setting and stitch, pulling the end in front of you as it goes through the machine. This gives an attractive stretchy cord which is ideal as a trimming, for straps, or which can be couched on to a fabric in an irregular manner to give texture.

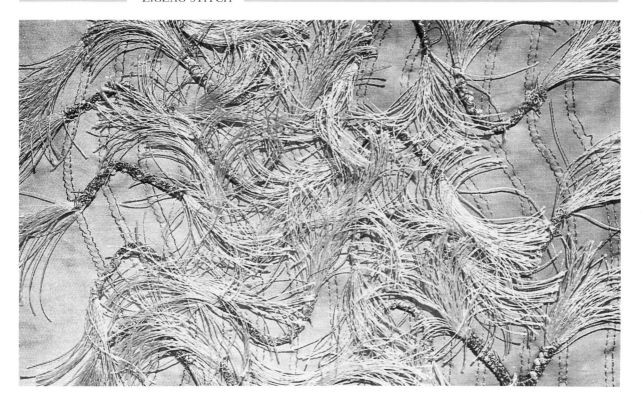

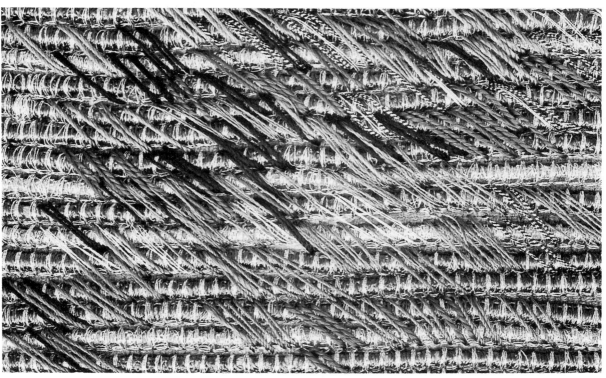

97 Top *Short lengths of wrapped yarns applied to a fabric decorated with twin-needle stitching.* DORRIT GRATER.

98 Above *Wrapped string was applied to a fabric using an automatic pattern. Hand stitches were then added in silk threads.*

Drawn thread work

This is often thought of as a hand embroidery technique, but it can be successfully worked on the machine using zigzag. How the threads are withdrawn and the fabric prepared depends very much on the purpose of the article, as the embroidery can be very formal and regular or completely random. Traditionally, an evenweave linen is used, but try one of the modern furnishing fabrics where threads can be pulled out easily. Frame the fabric and snip and withdraw groups of threads horizontally and vertically. Set the machine to the widest zigzag, and use a thread colour to blend with the fabric, as it is the spaces rather than the stitching, which are the feature of the work. Stitch over the remaining groups of threads in lines, either regularly or by moving the frame in small jerks from side to side to catch in threads from adjoining groups. This is easier with the foot removed and the feed dog lowered, but for a formal effect the foot and feed dog can be in position. The only problem is that the foot has to be removed and replaced each time you take the frame from the machine. More stitchery is often required to neaten the bands, and you can go over them again and again until quite a firm result is achieved. Lines of stitching can be continued on to the solid fabric, and this helps to tie in the snipped ends of the withdrawn threads. Worked areas can also be cut out and applied to another fabric with more stitching. Ribbons or fabric rouleaux can be woven through the bands of stitching, or ribbons knotted at the intersections.

Top tension	-- Normal to tight
Bobbin tension	-- Normal
Presser foot	-- Off
Feed dog	-- Lowered or covered
Stitch length	-- 0
Stitch width	-- Wide
Fabric	-- Framed
Needle size	-- 90

99 *Drawn thread worked in silver on space-dyed scrim, woven with ribbons sponged with the same colours. Very narrow ribbons were woven and knotted in.*

Drawn fabric work

Again this is often seen as a hand technique, and many machine embroiderers produce their first sample of drawn fabric quite accidentally by zigzag stitching on a loosely woven fabric such as scrim. Even with normal tensions, zigzag or satin stitch tends to pull the threads of the fabric together into groups, leaving a lacy pattern of holes. Where this is done deliberately an attractive and strong fabric is produced, as no threads are removed to weaken the fabric. Scrim is ideal for a first experiment. Frame the fabric and very slightly increase the top tension. Working freely, let the stitches build up in blobs in some parts and more openly in others, gathering in threads of the background fabric as you stitch.

100 *Tailor-tacking loops used as an insertion stitch between strips of silk noil decorated with sponging over drops of candle wax. The edges are turned to the right side and frayed, and ribbons are woven through the loops.*

Tailor tacking or looping foot

A tailor tacking or embroidery looping foot has a bar which projects upwards between the toes of the foot and over which the top thread has to loop as the machine stitches from side to side. These loops slip off at the back as you stitch, leaving a raised pile. Your machine may have a tailor tacking foot supplied as a standard fitting, but if not, ask your dealer if there is one available for your model. Quite apart from their use for tailor tacking in dressmaking, the

Top tension	-- Normal to loose
Bobbin tension	-- Normal
Presser foot	-- Tailor tacking foot
Feed dog	-- Up
Stitch length	-- Any
Stitch width	-- Medium to wide
Fabric	-- Unframed
Needle size	-- 90

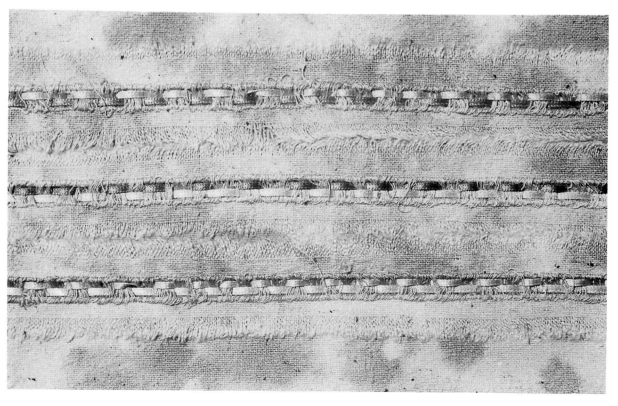

potential for textured pile areas in embroidery adds another stitch technique to your range. Since the loops are made by the foot, you obviously cannot remove the foot for free stitching, and straight or curved lines should be planned. If you frame the fabric and lower the feed dog, however, you will find that you can stitch fairly freely in any direction.

Insertions

Use this foot for insertion stitching as an open decorative seam. Prepare the two edges of the fabric by tacking a small hem or by fraying the edges and folding back the fraying to the right side. Hold the two folded edges together under the tailor tacking foot, set the machine for zigzag, and stitch to join the two edges together. Remove from the machine and pull the fabrics apart to flatten the loops. Metallic threads give a nice springy insertion, and with a slightly loose top tension try two threads through the needle for a thicker band of stitching. Ribbons are ideal for this technique and need no preparation of the edges. A band of ribbons joined with insertions could form the focal point on a fashion garment or bags and would be very individual if the ribbon had been previously sponged with fabric dyes, marbled or stitched with automatic patterns. Weave ribbons through the insertion stitches, or if you have a chain stitch machine, work rows of chain stitch down the insertion, giving an instant row of raised chain band.

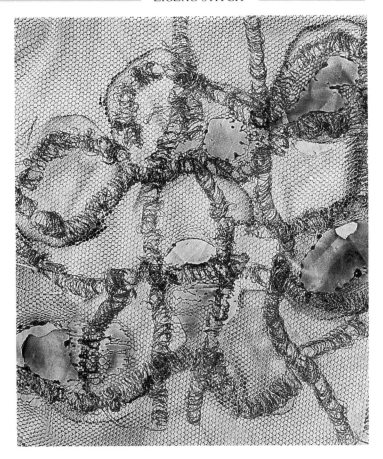

101 *Irregular lines of loops stitched over layers of fabric and net, with holes burnt in the net.*
DORRIT GRATER.

102 *Tailor-tacking loops used as insertion between strips of stitched fabric. The edges are frayed and folded back to the right side. A variegated red/yellow/blue/green thread was used for the stitching and the loops.*

Making a thread

Using the ribbon yarn which is sold for knitting, or ordinary narrow ribbon, stitch rows of tailor tacking or looping down the centre or on the edge, or both, to produce your own textured thread. If you cut a centimetre (half inch) wide strip of tights (pantyhose), cutting round and round the leg to give a long continuous strip, and tailor tack down the middle, pulling hard while you sew, you will find that the finished cord is still stretchy even when stitched. Couch down these cords to give textured areas, or weave them through an insertion seam already made with the tailor tacking foot.

Texture

With just a little experimentation, it is easy to become quite addicted to looping. With the fabric in a frame and the feed dog lowered, a rich area of loops can be worked over and over so that areas are flattened by still more loops. If you want to cut a row or area of loops to give a fringe, you must first back the fabric with iron-on interfacing, or the tufts can be pulled out. As with all zigzag techniques, practise altering the stitch length as you sew to give dense areas and spiky open areas.

103　*Detail of a quilted grey silk jacket with loops worked over applied ribbons. Diagonal bands of extra stitching and beads travel across the fabric.*

104　*Drawing of the jacket.*
LINDA RAKSHIT.

Satin Stitch

To anyone unfamiliar with machine embroidery, 'satin stitch' conveys automatically produced motifs or monograms, but as a stitch technique it is infinitely variable. Learn all you can about satin stitch on your machine. Select a firm fabric or two layers of fabric together and thread your machine with a different colour top and bottom. Sew rows of satin stitch, starting with the narrowest width and progressing through all the settings to the widest. Work rows just touching each other – this is a difficult technique to control, but practice does make perfect. Then try altering the stitch width as you sew, going from wide to narrow and back to wide. Close rows of this encroach on previous rows in parts and leave gaps of fabric in others.

Top tension	-- Normal to loose
Bobbin tension	-- Normal
Presser foot	-- Satin stitch foot
Feed dog	-- Up
Stitch length	-- Very short to long
Stitch width	-- Very narrow to wide
Fabric	-- Unframed
Needle size	-- 90

Altering the stitch length changes the density of the stitching so that, at the shortest stitch length, the fabric hardly seems to be moving, while with a longer stitch length zigzag results. The various qualities and thicknesses of threads require quite different stitch length adjustments to produce a smooth and pleasing effect. Alter both the stitch width and length as you sew. You will certainly feel as though you need an extra pair of hands but you will learn a great deal about satin stitch and confidence grows with practice. Work two lines of satin and then another line over the top down the middle. Sew a narrow row of satin over the middle of a row of the widest setting or a row of zigzag over a row of close satin. Many other variations are possible, just using the stitch width and stitch length dials and straight or slightly curved lines.

Tensions

Generally a slightly loose top tension is required for satin stitch. Otherwise the fabric puckers or the bobbin thread shows at the edge of the line. Of course

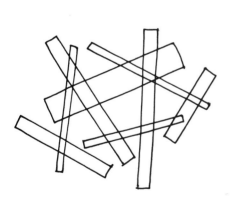

105 Above *Bands of satin stitch of varying widths, worked at different angles to build up a pattern.*

106 *The width of satin stitching can be altered as you work by turning the stitch width knob or moving the lever to give flowing patterns.*

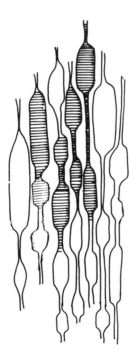

this effect may be to your liking, so try tightening the top tension to produce it deliberately. If puckering is a problem, reduce the top tension further, or back your work with paper or tear-away backing. Some bobbin cases have a small hole at the end of the finger and the manual recommends that the lower cotton is threaded through this for perfectly smooth satin stitch.

Threads

The range of modern threads is seen to full advantage with satin stitch. Matt cotton, shiny rayon, fine silks, mercerized cotton and the various man-made threads all give a different effect. Choose a colour range and collect together all the various fibre types you have, working close rows of them for reference. You will see which suits your machine, but generally the finest threads give the best results. Take time to get the stitch length just right for the thread you are using. Work massed lines with the shaded and variegated threads, and blocks of each colour will emerge. You need to work quite a large area of this to see if it is effective, and a more subtle colour blending results from using two threads

through the needle. Wind a bobbin with the variegated thread and put it on the spool pin with the reel of the same thread on top. The metallic threads look very rich in satin stitch, but remember to loosen the top tension even more when using them.

Fabrics

The nature of the fabric always alters the look of stitching and particularly so with satin stitch. On a textured furnishing fabric or felt the line sinks into the fabric, whereas on a firm cotton or satin the stitching looks almost raised. A lovely effect is produced on velvet, as the pile

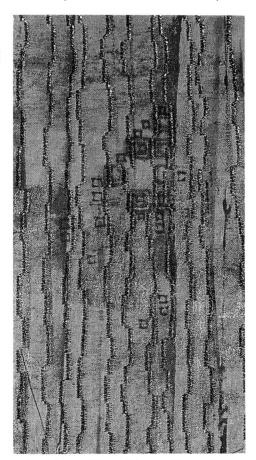

108 *The position of the needle can be altered from time to time to give breaks in the line. Here, the fabric was sponged with coloured paints before the stitching, and the small squares drawn in with a gold pen.*

107 *A design which can be worked with the presser foot on, and the width of the stitch altered as you go. Do not try to follow this exactly, but allow the fabric to move as it will.* LU BLEYBERG.

disappears under the stitching and you have the contrast of smooth lines with the texture of the velvet. You could work irregular horizontal and vertical lines of satin stitch so that little squares and rectangles of pile would show in the spaces, giving a velvet evening bag a whole new look and stiffening the fabric at the same time. On loosely woven fabric it is difficult not to produce drawn fabric with satin stitch, as described in the previous chapter. Striped and geometric-patterned fabrics offer possibilities for enrichment and it is even more rewarding to print your own fabric, using the edge of a piece of card brushed with fabric·paint, and add lines of satin stitch.

Patterns

As well as lines of satin stitch, work short lengths of stitching to give an all-over pattern on the fabric. Use lines of different width, some with close satin stitch and others as a more open zigzag, and position these at varying angles, crossing over each other or in a formal pattern. If you use a shiny thread for vertically and horizontally stitched blocks, a tonal change of colour will be seen. The ends of the thread can be taken to the back and fastened off, or a few straight stitches worked to connect each block of stitching – thus forming part of the pattern. The most modern machines have up to five different needle positions, and this gives a delightful broken pattern on satin stitching, difficult to obtain by moving the fabric yourself.

Corners

Sometimes your design will demand corners in satin stitch, and the diagram shows how these can be worked. Practise all of them and then decide which method appeals to you or suits the design. It would be fun to try a log cabin patchwork pattern worked entirely in satin stitch.

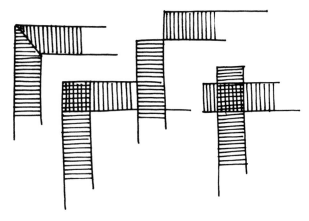

109   *Diagrams of the types of corners possible when using satin stitch – butted, overlapped and mitred.*

110   *Sample of satin stitch patterns in silver thread on striped silk, showing some corners.*

Corduroy fabrics

This seems an obvious fabric for satin stitch. The samples show solid bands of stitching with each row of satin stitch covering the line of fabric pile. The first row is easy, but subsequent adjoining rows are more difficult because the presser foot slips on the stitching of the previous row. Overcome this by holding the fabric at each side of the foot, with the palm of your hands flat on the fabric and slightly pulling each side away from the foot. It is easier to see the 'ditches' in the fabric if you stitch with the nap running away from you.

III   *Bands of satin stitching in grey, ivory and silver on white corduroy, with added lines of silver whip stitch between them. The fabric was then cut and woven, sewn into strips, and folded to make a chevron band. These textures and patterns could be used on cushions.*

Edges

Your sewing machine manual will give practical hints for oversewing edges. Adjust the stitch width and stitch length to suit the fabric type and guide the edge of the fabric to the centre of the foot so that the needle goes into the fabric and then over the edge. Use the overlocking foot to give perfect smooth edges. If both sides are to be visible, keep the tensions normal so that the stitch interlocks on the outer edge. However, if only the top side is to show, slightly loosen the top tension so that the stitch will interlock on the underside. Place the cut edge of the fabric on a piece of tear-away backing and stitch through both before tearing the backing away. A really decorative edge is made by folding a strip of tights (pantyhose) and stitching along the folded edge, pulling hard while you sew. The

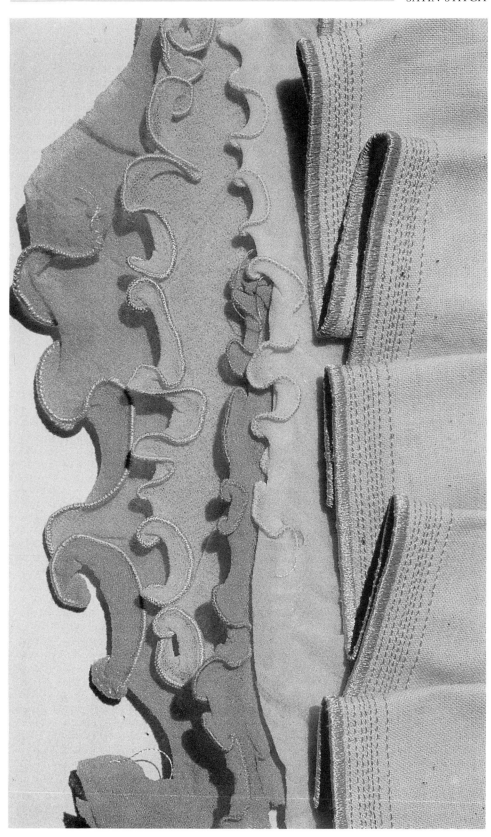

A smooth satin stitch edge on calico contrasts with the fluted edges worked on a stretch fabric.

satin stitch will curl and turn on itself. A similar edge can be made on the knitted jersey fabric used for T-shirts, and is far too attractive to be on the inside on the garment.

113 *Detail of a sleeve decoration, combining triangles printed with strips of card, and overlapping lines of satin stitch making larger triangles. The fabric in the centre was cut away and the holes are backed with further stitching. The colours are peach, yellow and coral on cream fabric.*

Cutwork

Satin stitch has always been associated with cutwork, either by hand or machine. Choose a closely woven fabric, both to support the stitchery and to produce neat cut edges. Make sure your design does not include large shapes to be cut, as the stitched edges will sag in use. The tensions should be normal so that the stitches interlock on the edge. Begin with simple or geometric designs and work all the satin stitch before you cut the spaces. If the edges look a little ragged, work another line of satin stitch to neaten and strengthen them.

114 *A similar pattern for cutwork. The dark areas will be cut away.*

1 *'In the Hot House – Watch the Tiger.' Machine quilted collage using velvets, satins and organdie.* Paddy Killer (formerly Ramsey). *Owned by Shipley Art Gallery, Gateshead, Contemporary Craft Collection.*

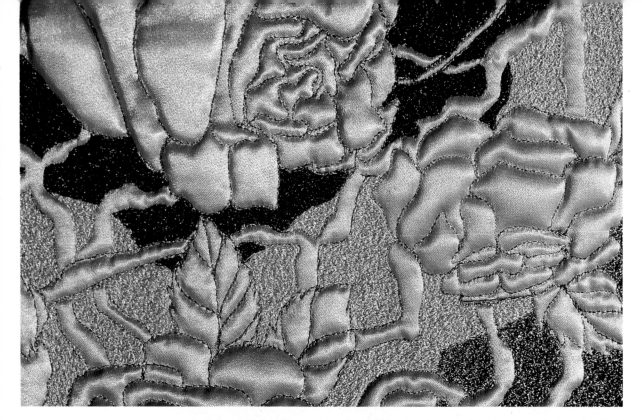

2 *Detail of roses showing granite stitch used to throw padded areas into relief.*
Paddy Ramsey.

3 *Two bags made with solid stitching in two directions which totally covers the fabric and gives the impression of weaving.*
Valerie Campbell-Harding.

4 *Machine-wrapped threads stitched together to make a grid, laid over stitching on hand-made paper. Fabrics are crumple-painted, stitched in layers and slashed; pieces are made by stitching across holes and applied; squares and rectangles are applied over free satin stitching with more stitching over them; and ruched and stitched lamé is added.* Marian Murphy.

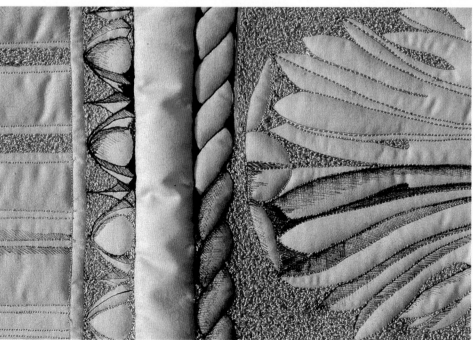

5 *Detail showing drawing on calico with a fine technical pen with granite stitch used to throw padded areas into relief.* Paddy Ramsey.

6 LEFT *'The Spanish Lady'.* Solid stitching in irregular areas, with the stitching so distorting the fabric that the embroidery has a folded and undulating surface, planned to emphasize particular areas of the design. Alice Kettle.

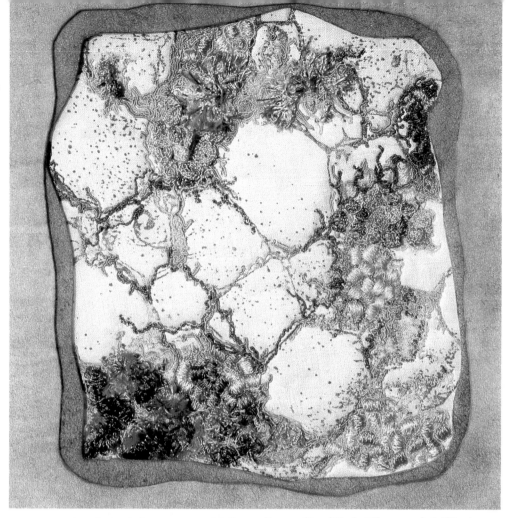

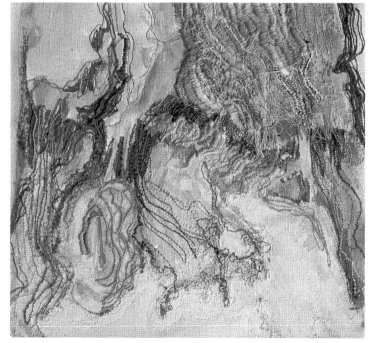

7 ABOVE *'Paved Garden'.* Photocopy of a bubble print heat-transferred to silk fabric with whip stitch, looping and satin stitch blobs. Pamela Watts.

8 *Embroidery based on drawing of threads in a storage jar. Free running stitch, whip stitch and zigzag stitching.* Val Du Cros.

11 RIGHT *Detail of a panel based on drawings of Japanese armour. Black velvet applied to black cotton, painted and streaked with copper and gold powders. Straight strips of fabric are distorted with stitching to give the twisted shapes which are wrapped with machine-made cords. Extra whip stitch is added to blend these into the background.* Valerie Campbell-Harding.

9 *'Blue Spike Hat.' Exotic fabric and threads are sandwiched between layers of transparent plastic with machine embroidery. A variety of softer textures such as dyed or painted felt or velvet are added, and then machine-embroidered, leaving part of the background exposed.* Judy Clayton.

10 *Printed background covered in parts with organdie. Tonal areas built up with scraps of nets, scrim and calico secured with free running and zigzag stitching.* Julia Clough.

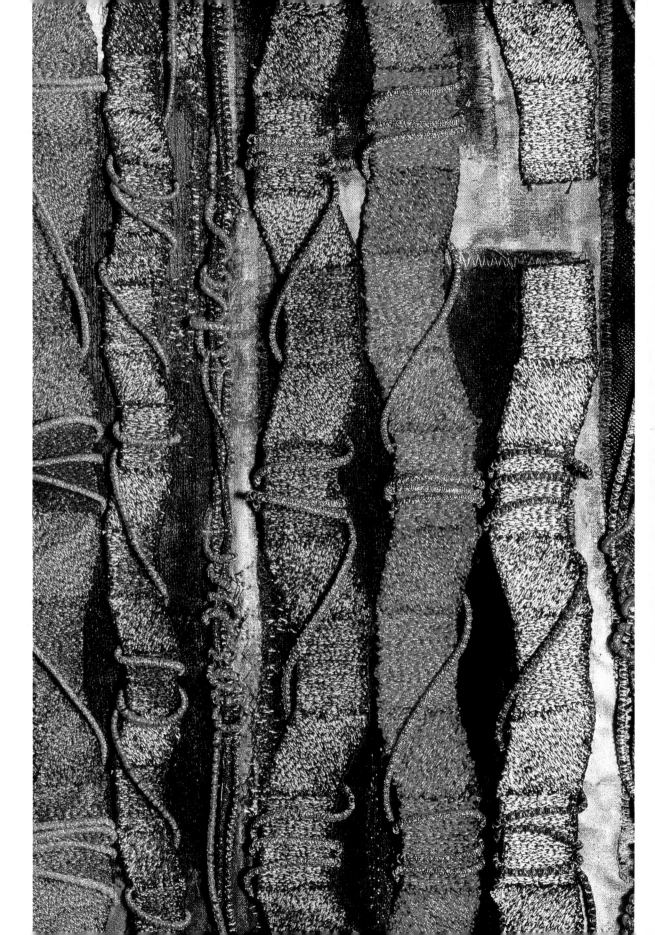

12 *Detail of a panel with applied squares of previously stitched fabric, blended into the background with zigzag whip stitch.* Christine Cook.

13 *Silver and gold leathers applied as a background to the coloured flowers which were stitched with coloured threads in different directions. The leathers were stitched in silver and gold thread to break up the shine.* Linda Rakshit.

14 *Threads bonded onto silk with lines of free satin stitch.* Pamela Watts.

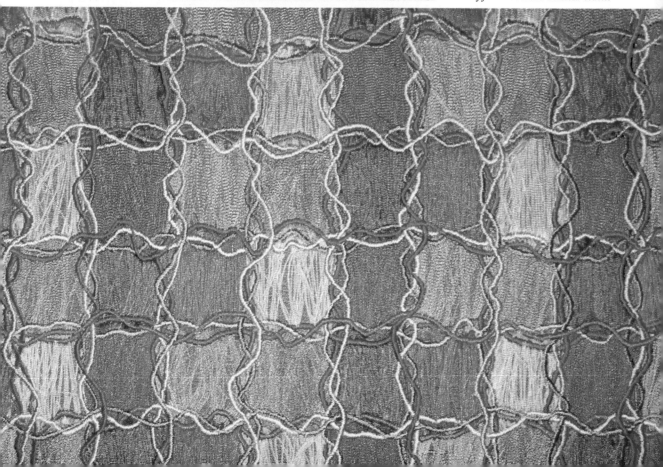

17 *Detail of panel.* Christine Cook.

16 *Layers of shot nylon organza tacked onto hot-water–*
dissolve fabric with free running stitch worked over the edges.
These are mounted to hang in layers on a box construction. Two
layers of stippled silk organza were bonded together and burnt
into ivy leaf shapes and attached to cover the top and sides of the box.
Margaret Ross.

15 LEFT *Four*
lozenges of black
felt and fabric
machined solidly to
give an undulating
surface, with added
couching. Applied
to black muslin, slit,
with zig-zagged
edges.
Christine Cook.

18 ABOVE *'Hand Jewellery.' Layered squares of tea-dyed silk organza, gold lamé and felt, decorated with eyelets and free running stitch. The squares are joined by wrapped washers.* Marion Brookes.

19 BELOW *Whip stitch used as a contrast to long straight stitches worked by hand over padding. The design used folded strips of paper on a painted background. The pattern and texture of the paint suggested the flowing lines of stitching.* Linda Rakshit.

20 *Necklace combining separate pieces of machine embroidery, marbled gold threads and leather, with extra stitching and curled pieces of marbled plastic.* Julie Smith.

21 *Fabric printing leaving letters in silhouette with some background areas enriched with whip stitch.* Val du Cros.

22 *Ink drawing of sheep on calico, embellished with hand and machine stitching.* Jean Mould.

23 *Three bags based on a theme of bows, worked from a computer design. Loose whip stitch, cutwork and wrapped string cords.* Corliss Miller.

24 *Samples of zigzag stitching on painted graph paper. Holes were torn in some places.* Alison Elliott.

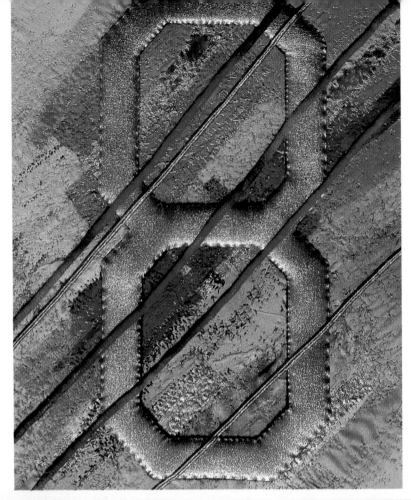

25 *Detail of an altar frontal based on the design shown in fig. 197. Pieces of applied fabric with zigzag whip stitch, padded gold kid and couched Russia braid with threaded ribbon yarn.* Christine Cook.

26 *Landscape worked on dark fabric with gold car paint spray, and areas emphasized with free running stitch using gold threads.* Anne Robinson.

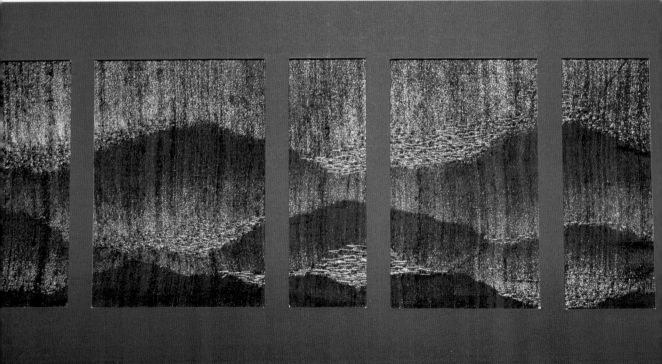

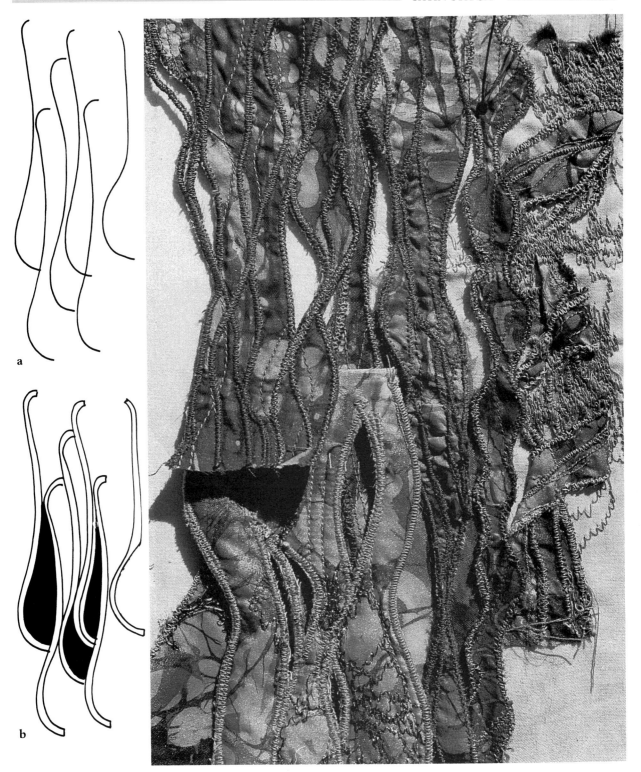

115(a) *A curved design built up from drawing around part of a spoon*
(b) *The lines are doubled for satin stitch and the black areas will be cut away.*

116 *Cutwork sample on batik, using flowing curves to give movement.*
ROS ARNO.

Satin stitch blobs

Select a very short stitch length and a medium or long stitch width and work satin stitch so that the stitches build up solidly and the finished blob is more or less square. Raise the presser foot, and with the needle in its highest position move the fabric ready for the next blob. You may find that this is easier if the fabric is framed, and check by turning the fly wheel towards you that the position of the needle is correct for the next stitch. The top thread will lie on the surface joining the blobs, and you will see from the diagram that these can be arranged to form many different patterns.

Alternatively, work running stitch all round the blobs to cover the single thread and form an attractive all-over pattern. You may prefer to work this technique as free stitching.

118 *Sample worked on calico with applied pieces of pelmet interfacing which has had holes punched out with a leather punch. Secured with massed satin stitch blobs, using a variegated thread to give a rich and crunchy texture.*

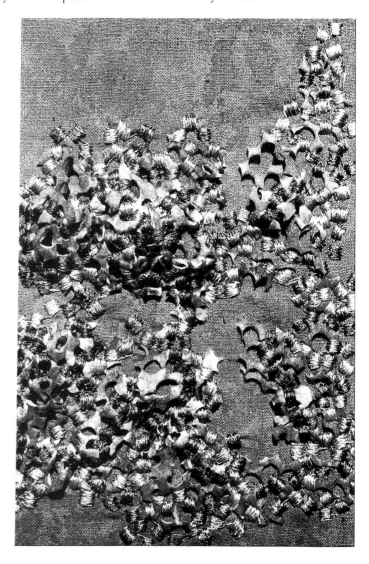

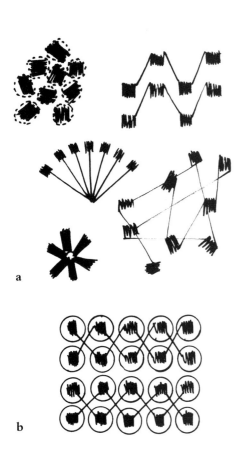

a

b

117(a) *Satin stitch blobs can be worked to build up many patterns.*
(b) *Circles of pelmet interfacing, cut with a leather punch, and secured with a satin stitch blob in the centre of each.*

Free satin stitch

Most of the satin stitch techniques described so far in this chapter show the characteristic of smooth stitching associated with satin. With the presser foot removed and the feed dog lowered, however, much more movement and texture is possible. The diagrams give suggestions for gaining control and confidence with free satin stitch. Now that the frame can be moved in all directions, select the widest stitch width and practise moving the frame sideways. This gives an entirely different effect, with horizontal lines of long stitches. Continue stitching in lines, curves and circles. Let

Top tension	-- Normal to loose
Bobbin tension	-- Normal
Presser foot	-- Off
Feed dog	-- Lowered or covered
Stitch length	-- 0
Stitch width	-- Wide
Fabric	-- Framed
Needle size	-- 90

the stitches build up in areas by moving the frame slowly sideways, towards and away from you. Stitch one colour into another and do try the shaded threads, as this is a case where they can be used to great advantage.

119 *Samples of some of the patterns possible using satin stitch to make solid areas of stitching, flowing shapes, cross shapes and grid patterns. Satin stitch blobs or beads can be cut to give a pile surface.*

120 *A design which could be worked in satin stitch.*

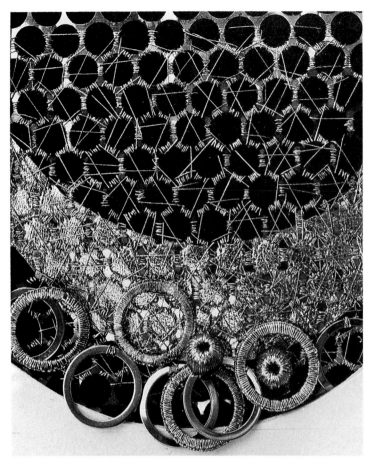

Holding objects down

Inspiration can be found all around the house for this technique. Cut thin strips of card, pelmet interfacing or pieces of sequin waste, and satin stitch over them on to a background fabric, covering it either completely or just in parts. If you are using fabric printing, do print the card or interfacing at the same time as the fabric, as this helps to integrate the two together. So many things can be stitched over – think of toothpicks or DIY tile spacers. Perhaps it is wise to practise on soft things, as it is possible to break a needle by hitting something hard.

121 *Sequin waste held to a backing of silk and gold leather, with satin stitch in a variegated metal thread. Buttonholed rings give a contrast.*

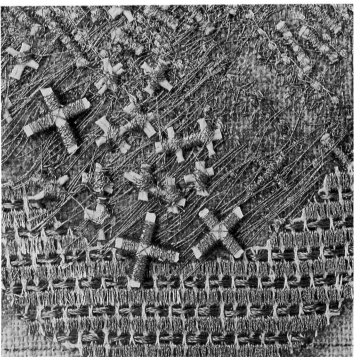

122 *Satin stitch used to hold down short lengths of string, small cut pieces of rug canvas and plastic tile spacers, on a background of long stitches (see 'Long stitches', page 102).*

Padded satin stitch

This is a useful technique to give emphasis to a line or area in a design. A narrow row of satin stitch can be stitched over with a wider one. Alternatively, use a firm string and stitch it down with zigzag to hold it in place while you check that it is what you want. Then go over it with close satin stitch, letting the stitches build up really densely in parts to accentuate areas of the design. Collect together many different weights of string and cord and stitch them down to see the contrast between quite fine padded lines and really thick ones.

123 Below *Wider over narrower satin stitch gives a slightly raised line, in blues, mauves and pinks on cream fabric.*

124 *Satin stitch over string gives a very raised line which contrasts with sideways zigzag.*

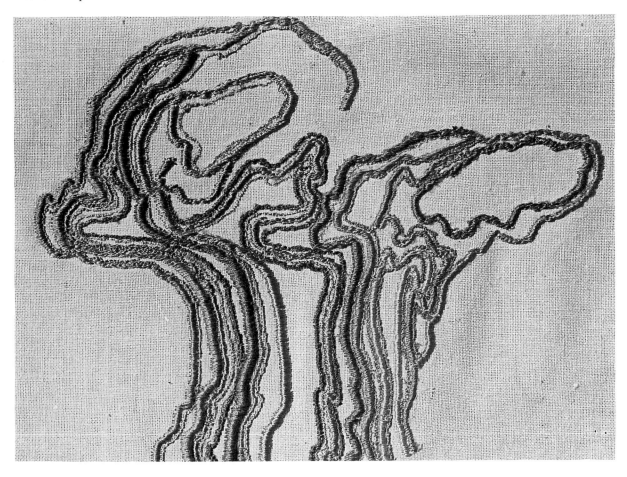

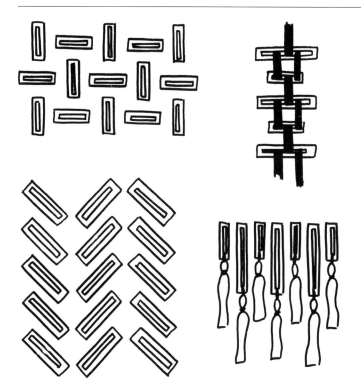

Buttonholes

It is a great shame that buttonholes are thought of as functional, as their use as decoration is far more interesting. Developments in sewing machine technology make buttonholes easy and perfect every time. The latest computerized machines have a memory, so that buttonholes of identical length can be repeated, and keyhole and corded varieties are possible too. Whatever your model of machine, read the manual and try buttonholes on different fabrics and with a variety of threads – this will be useful practice for dressmaking purposes too. Then forget about practicalities and work through some of the following suggestions.

- Work buttonholes on felt, pelmet interfacing, leather or fabric, which is then frayed back to the stitching. Cut out and reapply at various angles, stitching down with a few satin stitches on to little squares of translucent fabric or a printed background fabric.

125 *Suggestions for patterns which can be built up using buttonholes. The holes can be slit, and ribbon or braid woven through, or the bases can be decorated with tassels.*

126 *Buttonholes worked on pelmet interfacing, cut out and applied to fabric over frayed pieces of organza.*

- Work buttonholes all along a strip of fabric or wide ribbon, and button on to the main fabric purely as decoration. This looks lovely down the sleeve of a blouse, with the strip prettily edged with curling satin stitch. Can also be used as band decoration on a cushion, or for bags.
- Apply a strip of buttonholes to a main fabric with tufting, made with the looping foot, coming out of the slits.
- Make band or chevron patterns of buttonholes and thread ribbons or cords through or add little tassels at the ends (or both).
- Use a gimp cord, recommended for strengthening the buttonhole, and instead of cutting the ends off, leave them as frayed tufts for decoration.
- Where buttonholes are really needed, work many more than required on both edges. Thread strips of fabric, rouleaux or cords through to fasten. A decorative version of the corset and much used in Elizabethan clothing.

The main attraction of this approach is the element of surprise – one buttonhole is functional; lots become fun.

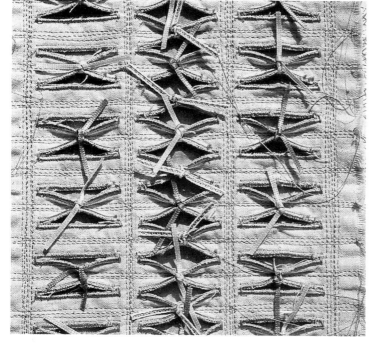

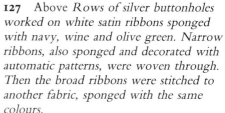

127 Above *Rows of silver buttonholes worked on white satin ribbons sponged with navy, wine and olive green. Narrow ribbons, also sponged and decorated with automatic patterns, were woven through. Then the broad ribbons were stitched to another fabric, sponged with the same colours.*

128 *Rows of buttonholes held open with knots of narrow ribbon, showing coloured silk underneath.*

Automatic patterns

An approach similar to that used for buttonholes is required for automatic patterns. Many of the latest machines have a bewildering array of patterns, either built in or inserted as cams, and ranging from practical stitches, to rows of flowers and leaves, to dogs. The manuals show single lines of pattern, but we think you will see from the samples that there is much more to it than that for the embroiderer. Work through the range of stitches on your machine, using different threads, two threads through the needle or metal threads. Try working a line of pattern over a wide row of satin stitch. Then set your machine for whip or cable

129 *Automatic patterns are worked in lines holding down strips of frayed fabric, ribbons and cut lengths of pre-stitched ribbon.*

stitch, and immediately the set pattern will look very different. Whatever effect you choose, work close or overlapping rows to build up an area of stitching. Automatic patterns can be opened out or 'stretched' on some machines. On others they can be altered by increasing or decreasing the stitch length and stitch width. They can be worked continuously as patterned texture or in disconnected short bursts. Some machines will stitch a single motif which can be placed as random pattern, rather than a line. The needle position can be changed while stitching, which alters the pattern. Work lines on strips of felt or ribbons and knot, plait, weave or thread them through buttonholes or large eyelets. Do build up the background with paint or dyes, other fabrics or stitchery, just as you would with other techniques, and keep changing the colour of the threads to add interest.

Your machine manual will tell you how

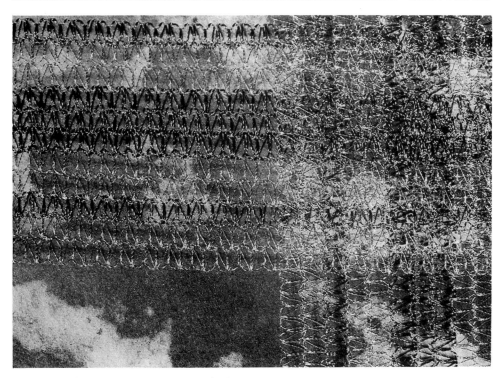

130 Top *An automatic pattern worked in two directions to give extra density at the corner.*

to match patterns exactly and how to turn corners perfectly. We think it is more important to use your imagination when working with these patterns and not to aim for the perfect result.

131 Right *Scallop pattern used as an edging on fabrics, built up in layers. The painted papers were stitched with the same pattern, which perforated the paper so that it could easily be pulled apart, giving a scalloped edge.*

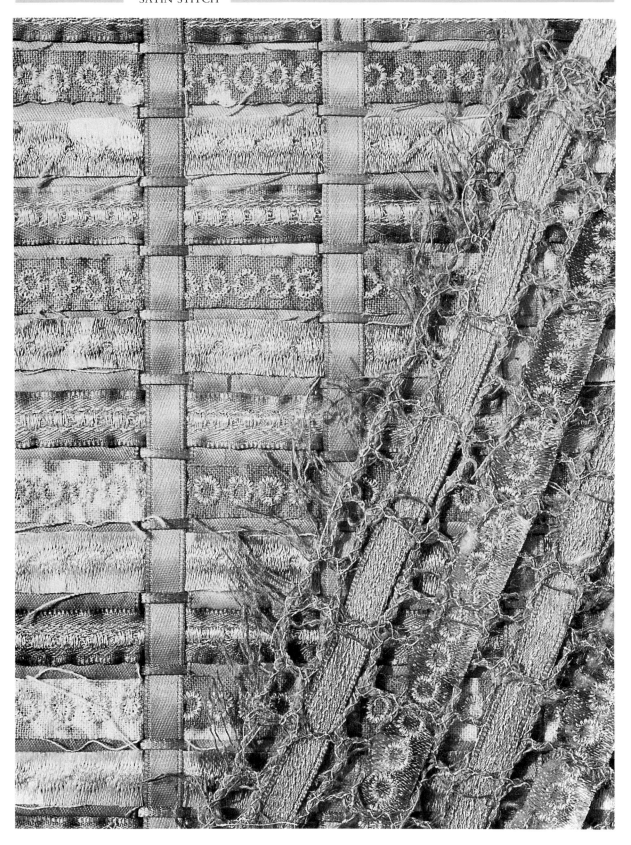

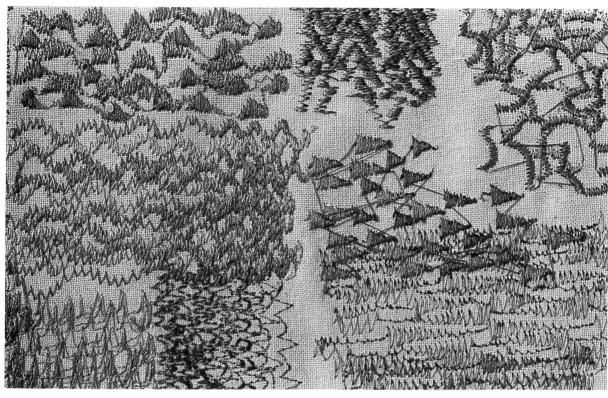

132 Left *Two samples showing space-dyed ribbons decorated with automatic patterns; one woven through drawn thread work and the other woven with plain ribbons.*

133 Below *Single units of automatic patterns used irregularly to create pattern and texture.*

134 Above *Lines of satin stitch worked on thin strips of painted calico. The fabric was frayed back to the stitching and the lines secured, in layers, with an automatic pattern on top of the satin stitch.*

135 *A bag made from plaited strips of fabric, previously decorated with lines of automatic pattern. The plaits shade from dark red to pink, stitched with silver. Wrapped cocktail sticks with added tassels give movement in use.* LINDA RAKSHIT.

Making a fabric with automatic patterns

Print or sponge bands of colour on a fabric using fabric paints, or apply strips of sheer fabrics with iron-on bonding fabric. Choose one of your machine patterns, and stitch overlapping lines really densely. Add lines of running stitch and then more lines of automatic pattern. (It would be interesting to work some of the lines, apply the sheer fabrics on top, and then continue to work the chosen pattern.)

Using either the hot- or cold-water soluble fabric as a base, stitch solidly with automatic patterns, working both horizontal and vertical lines. Add running stitch and make sure the finished piece is densely stitched and interlocked before dissolving the base in water. The resulting fabric is surprisingly strong and could be used as an insert for fashion items.

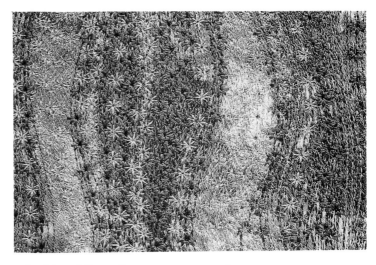

136 *Massed lines of a star pattern together with lines of running stitch, built up to make a rich fabric.*

137 *The same pattern stitched over a straight-stitch grid on water-soluble fabric, to make a lacy material.* LINDA RAKSHIT.

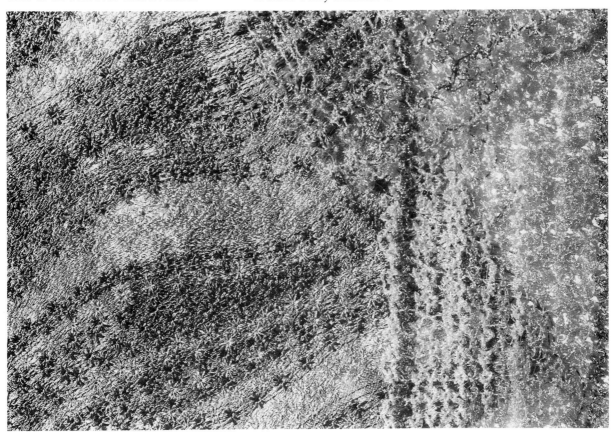

Eyelets

Ask your dealer whether your machine has eyelet plates as an accessory, as these are one of the most useful additions for embroidery. They are sometimes listed as 'English embroidery' plates and are available in different sizes.

Use a fine thread and make a hole with a stiletto in a firm fabric which has been framed. Practise using different stitch widths on satin stitch setting and stitching round the hole closely or with just a few stitches for a spiky star eyelet. The nicest effect comes from overlapping and grouping different-sized eyelets together. Do not cut the stitch between eyelets, or the stitching will unravel. The fabric changes the nature of the eyelets considerably. On a loosely woven or sheer fabric the hole tends to distort and enlarge and the stitching pulls the fabric, but this may suit your design. On felt, however, lovely solid eyelets seem almost to sink into the fabric.

138 *Eyelets worked using the eyelet attachment on two different machines. The underneath sample has extra rings of stitching around the outer edge of some eyelets.*

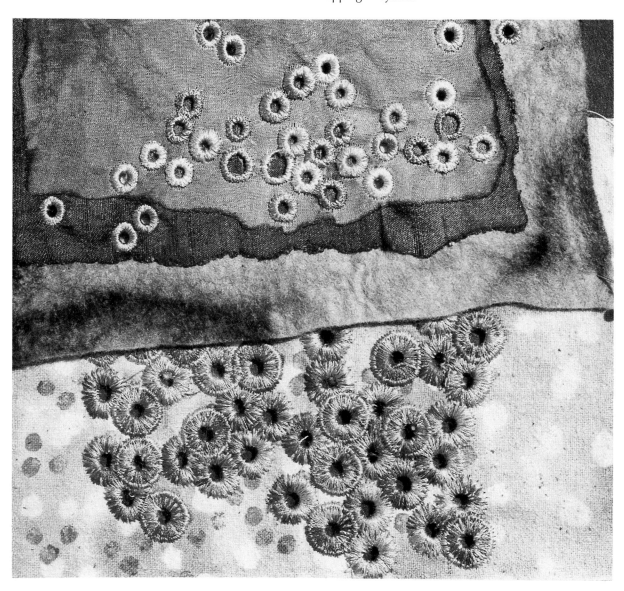

6 Further Developments of Stitch Techniques

The preceding chapters on techniques are not intended to be the whole story but rather to serve as instruction and, we hope, inspiration. As we worked on each stitch many new lines of experimentation occurred to us. We became so excited as each idea led to another that many times we thought we would never finish one chapter, let alone the book. We describe here some of these developments and feel sure that you will already have discovered some of your own. They are not necessarily 'advanced' techniques, but rather a natural progression of confidence and learning.

From our own experience, the first requirement for fruitful experimentation is to set yourself a particular stitch technique and determine to master every aspect. It is so easy to alter the tensions for whip stitch and regard the matter conquered, or to wind a bobbin with thick thread and tick off cable stitch. When the time comes to stop practising and to work a design, it is the subtle control of a stitch and its variations which will make for a sensitive interpretation.

So select lots of different fabrics, organize your threads and try every single way you can think of to work that stitch. Look really carefully at the textures and patterns you are making and take time to change colours and threads.

The following pages represent some of our 'developments', and we hope that these will inspire many more of your own.

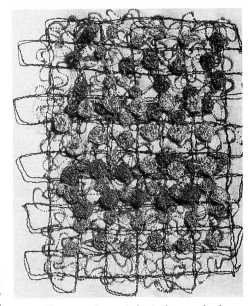

140 *Free running stitch circles worked on mesh, secured to fabric with a grid pattern of stitching.* SARAH WEBB.

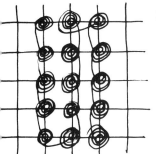 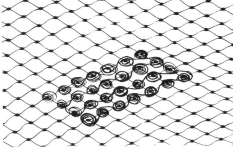

139 *Diagrams showing free running stitch worked around the intersections of a square and diamond mesh.*

Stitching on mesh

Many supermarkets sell fruit and vegetables in plastic mesh bags. Instead of throwing these away, cut off the ends and along one side so that you have a flat piece of mesh. Use a small ring frame and try to pull the mesh as tight as possible. Use free running to stitch round and round the intersection of the mesh, building up raised blobs. Move to the next intersection, vary the size of the blobs and try to cover all the mesh by making the edges of the circles touch each other. Choose the colour of the bobbin thread with care, as this shows as much as the top thread. Work an area, cut away the outer area of mesh and apply to another fabric. It is quite pliable and can be sewn down to give a raised and crunchy look. Experiment with weaving and threading strips of fabric through the mesh or adding hand stitching on top of the machined circles.

Making a fabric

Possibly because free running is a simple stitch, it seems to offer endless scope. We started by wrapping threads in a figure of eight round a card window mount and stitching backwards and forwards to hold them as a braid-like strip. (Think of the base threads as the warp and the machining as the weft.) By extending this principle, a whole new fabric can be made with complete control of colour and texture. The card mount works reasonably well, but it tends to bend like a boomerang as the stitching progresses, especially if it is fairly large. A rigid square frame, thin enough to pass under the needle, is required. This can be made quite simply at home with four strips of metal, strong wire, really rigid plastic or even long lollipop sticks, held tightly together at the four corners with rubber bands. Wrap the base threads both horizontally and vertically, and work running stitch to secure all the threads together. Dense stitching will make a firm fabric, or you can leave more of the wrapped threads showing for a lacy look. When the work is complete, take off the rubber bands and pull out the four framing strips. The remaining loops can be left as part of the fabric, cut to form a fringe, or concealed in a seam. You can choose textured or metallic

141 *Diagrams showing various ways of making a fabric based on machined threads. Free running stitch can be worked over a group of threads held tightly under the needle, or threads can be wrapped round square frames in different ways.*

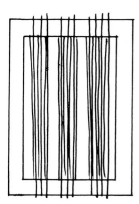
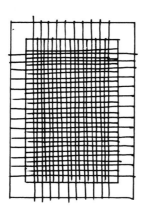
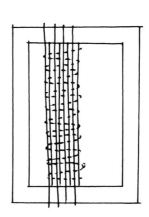

threads for the base, play with colour mixing, or leave square holes in the original thread wrapping. A whole design can be planned, part worked as the base and appliqué, cable, looping stitch etc. added, as you wish.

142 *A bag made using the wrapped fabric described on page 96, decorated with braids made by the same method. The wrapped yarn is a delicate filmy knitting ribbon, and the stitching is worked with a variegated metal thread.*
VALERIE CAMPBELL-HARDING.

Stitching across space – flowers

Frame a piece of calico and draw circles of approximately 3–4 cm ($1\frac{1}{4}$–$1\frac{3}{4}$ in.) diameter with a pencil. These can be freehand, slightly irregular and 1 cm ($\frac{1}{2}$ in.) apart. Set your machine for free running stitch and cut out one fabric circle on the drawn line. Lower the needle into the fabric half a cm from the cut edge and stitch straight across the space and into the fabric at the other side. Continue stitching close lines backwards and forwards, radiating all round the circle, until the middle is quite solid. When it is complete, cut the next fabric circle and stitch as before; continue cutting and sewing until all the circles on the frame are worked. Cut the threads all round the circle inside the fabric edge and a flower will appear, with spiky fringed edges and a solid stitched middle. Resist the temptation to cut out each flower as it is worked, or to cut all the circles at the beginning, or you will lose the tension in the frame and stitching will be difficult. Working one at a time, the stitching replaces the circular hole and the tension is maintained. These flowers are lovely to work using subtly shaded or metal threads. Apply different sized flowers with a few stitches through the middle, in massed areas. It might seem possible to work this technique with the presser foot on and the feed dog up or with reduced foot pressure, but stitching across space can upset the timing on some machines. To be on the safe side, always remove the presser foot and lower the feed dog.

143 *Diagrams showing square and round cut holes, filled with free running stitch in horizontal and vertical lines for squares and radiating lines for circles. The stitching should be cut away just inside the fabric edge.*

144 *A massed area of flowers secured to a background fabric, with free running stitch in the centres. Stitched over round holes using variegated threads in the bobbin and on the spool.*

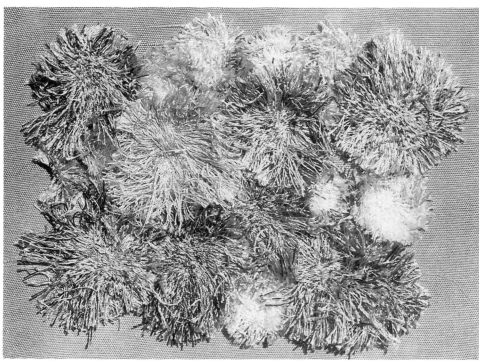

Stitching across space – edges

This follows the same principle as the flowers but gives a fabric edge fringed with stitching. It can be very practical for fashion, left uncut as an insertion band or used as interpretation for landscape. Frame a fabric and set your machine for free running stitch. Draw two straight or curved lines, parallel and about 1–2 cm ($\frac{3}{8}$–$\frac{3}{4}$ in.) apart, and stopping a little way in from the sides of your frame. Cut along these lines and between them at the ends so that you have a long thin rectangular hole. Lower the needle into the fabric and stitch to the edge of the hole, over the space and into the fabric at the other side. Machine backwards and forwards, and remember that the stitching on the fabric is going to show, so try to make it an attractive part of the design. Run the machine fairly fast and move the frame slowly especially when crossing over the hole. When you have stitched all the length of the hole, remove the fabric from the frame and

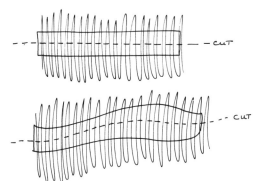

cut straight through the ends of the fabric and through the middle of the row of unsupported stitching. You now have two pieces of fabric, each edged with fringed stitching. The colour of the bobbin thread is important; this will not show on the fabric stitching but will be seen in the fringing. You can apply one fringed edge beneath the other for instant landscape effects, using running stitch to hold and integrate the two together. There are many possibilities for this technique – try a sample to help you decide how you want to use it.

145 *Diagrams showing straight and curved areas cut into fabric, with free running stitch worked across the spaces. Cut the unsupported stitching where indicated.*

146 *Below Landscape, built up in layers, using fabric stitched with fringing extending over the fabric edge. Free running stitch was added to integrate the layers. Worked on printed and painted calico.*

Stitching to distort

This is an exciting and satisfying way to work and gives an effect like no other. The distortion is in fact quite controllable and results from really dense stitching, deliberately used to make the surface and edges flute, wave and dome. Take a piece of calico about 5–7 cm (2–3 in.) square and place a piece of felt, the same size, underneath. Using the darning foot, lower the feed dog, change your needle to a size 100 or even 110 and use one or two threads through the needle. Put the two layers of fabric under the needle and stitch free running backwards and forwards, over and over again, until the needle will hardly pass through the fabric. Work encroaching blocks of stitching in different directions all over the background. When near an edge, stitch just over it and back on to the fabric again so all the cut edges are secured. You have probably finished when you can no longer see a single speck of the original fabric and the needle refuses to penetrate the stitching. Remember to clean the bobbin area of your machine after working this technique, as the dense stitching on the felt produces large quantities of fluff.

147 *Massed stitching radiating from the centres of these circles causes distortion of the whole piece. A single circle at the corner shows how radiating lines, if worked solidly enough, cause the edges to flute.*

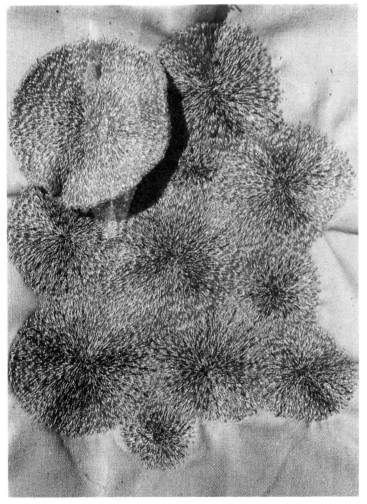

148 *Different patterns which cause distortion if the stitching is heavily massed. The scallop border pattern in the centre is very effective if worked on the edge of a piece.*

Controlling the distortion

Stitching in different directions alters the nature of the distortion, and stitches on small fabric shapes distort more than areas of stitching within a larger piece. Put two threads together in the needle, as the denser the stitching, the greater the distortion, and always use two layers of firm fabric or fabric backed with felt. Distortion is more pronounced on the straight grain of the fabric, and bands of straight free running tighten the fabric in the same direction as the stitching, making it expand at right angles. Spiral stitching produces a bowl shape, whereas radiating stitches, towards and away from a central point, make waves. Lines of stitching around the edge of a shape and parallel to it raise the centre of the shape itself. This method opens up a new area of machine embroidery. It is no longer surface decoration, but the creation of a surface. Think of the potential for belts, bags, hats, tiny sculptured shapes for jewellery or hangings. Discount the one small disadvantage of this technique – you use a tremendous amount of thread.

149 Top *Samples of massed stitching causing distortion. Massed stitching in spirals produces a bowl shape.*

150 Right *Before stitching, the shape of this bag was a rectangle. The stitching was worked on cotton fabric, backed with felt. The darning foot was used, and two threads through the needle.*

Long stitches

Many machines have an extra-long stitch, often called a basting or tacking stitch in the manual. This feature is operated by the machine motor running as normal, but the needle penetrates the fabric only every three, five or even twelve stitches, giving a stitch length of between 1 and 5 cm. ($\frac{3}{8}$ and 2 in.). Remove the presser foot, lower the feed dog and set your machine for the basting stitch, following the instructions in your manual. Frame the fabric and sew long spiky stitches in all directions. These can be built up into dense blocks – particularly effective when using a thin shiny thread. Use the long stitch to go over strips of fabric or bundles of threads, and you can vary the length of the stitch exactly. Practise moving the frame from side to side and,

with a little experience, you will be able to judge when the next stitch is due.

For machines with a vertical bobbin, but which do not have a long stitch built into them, it is possible to buy a magic needle with two eyes. Insert it into the machine as usual but thread the top eye only. Set your machine to the longest stitch length it will do, with the feed dog up and normal tension. Work either a normal zigzag stitch or the blind hemming stitch. The needle sews on the left side only and skips those stitches made on the right. The long stitches can be radiated from a central point for flowers, adding a tight circle of free running stitch in the centres. Pattern the fabric with long stitches and add zigzag or satin stitch to hold them in places and to distort the long straight lines. This has an obvious application in depicting

151 Above *A pattern using long stitches held at the intersection with satin stitch blobs.*

152 *Very long tacking or basting stitches allowed to build up into dense bands, contrasted with free running stitch in different directions for the background.*

gardens and landscapes, for areas of tall grasses, and it would work well with two green threads of different shades through the needle together. The work must be laced over card or framed when completed, as the long stitches tend to sag when removed from the frame.

153 Right *A pattern of flowers worked in free basting stitch radiating from the centres.* JUDITH SMALLEY.

154 *Landscape using very long basting stitches built up in layers. Areas of running and whip stitch were worked into the long stitches.*

a

Sideways zigzag

When using two threads in the needle together, it is usually recommended that you pass one each side of the tension disc so that both threads are tensioned. If you pass both threads on the same side of the disc, you will find that one thread will stitch normally while the other makes loops. Try this on free zigzag, moving the frame from side to side to produce long stitches. Two metal threads used together can make this a very rich and highly textured technique.

155a & b Landscapes on painted calico with bands of zigzag worked sideways, using two slightly textured metallic threads through the needle. Both were placed on the same side of the tension disc to give a loopy surface. Zigzag, satin and free running stitch complete the designs.

b

156 Landscape of trees and bushes worked in sideways zigzag and running stitch, using metallic threads.
MARION BROOKES

Satin stitch on canvas

Craft shops and embroidery suppliers have many different types of canvas including synthetic, double and single mesh and rug canvas. Experiment with colouring the canvas with paint or dye, and use it as a base for machining. Remove the presser foot and lower the feed dog. Select a satin stitch width so the needle goes over one, two or more of the threads; or move the canvas slightly from side to side so that the needle goes into the holes and not the canvas. (Do use up your old blunt needles for this technique.) You may have to tighten the lower tension slightly to produce a smooth stitch on the surface. The stitching can be very regular in horizontal or vertical lines or freely worked with encroaching areas of colour. Some lines can be padded with string to give a raised area, and if the mesh is open enough, you can weave metal threads, cords or strips of fabric through. This technique makes a strong, firm and attractive result which can be purely decorative or would be ideal for bags and belts.

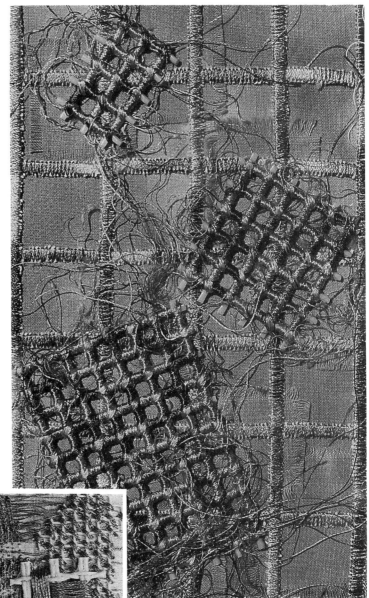

157 Above *Satin stitching on plastic rug canvas applied to a stitched grid over squares of painted fabric.*

158 *Long stitching on pieces of rug canvas, applied to tent stitch worked using satin stitch on the intersections of 14s canvas, contrasted with free whip stitch.*

Free eyelets

Not everyone has an eyelet attachment for their machine, and this alternative method gives results which can be fine and delicate or thick and crunchy, depending on the fabric you use and the amount of stitching worked. Use the darning foot and lower the feed dog. Set the stitch length at '0' and the stitch width to the widest your machine will allow. Keep the bobbin tension normal but loosen the top tension slightly. Frame a piece of organdie or silk organza and make holes in the fabric with a stiletto. Keep one edge of the hole near to the edge of the hole in the darning foot, work close zigzag around the hole in the fabric, with the stitches kept at right angles to the edge. Rotate the frame smoothly for an even eyelet, or work satin stitch blobs for a star shape. It takes some practice to keep the eyelet even, but a hole made in an organdie background stays open to make it easier, whereas with other fabrics it tends to close up.

An alternative method is to work eyelets on pelmet interfacing over punched holes. Using a leather or paper punch, make holes in a piece of pelmet interfacing. Set the machine as above and work a fine layer of zigzag around every hole. If you wish you can cut out an irregular shape to be applied to other stitchery by cutting close to the edge of

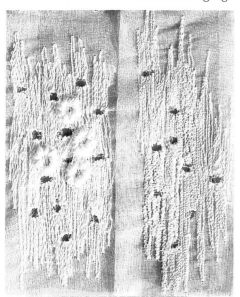

159 *Free eyelets made by punching holes in organdie with a stiletto and working to and fro between them.*

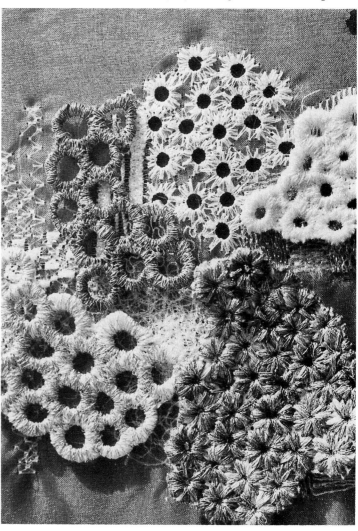

160 *Free eyelets made by punching a hole in organdie with a stiletto, or in pelmet interfacing with a paper punch; the fabric was then revolved while satin stitch was worked. The organdie was framed, the interfacing held with the fingers.*

the stitching. Work one or more layers of stitching around each hole, depending on how crunchy an effect you want. Start and finish the stitching with a few stitches on the spot, or some of the zigzag will unravel. Work slowly but steadily to avoid breaking the thread.

161 *'Walled Garden'. The fabric was printed with rubber stamps and pieces of sponge, and diagonal lines of stitching were worked over the whole piece. Free running stitch emphasized the stone wall and pieces of torn lace (made on water-soluble fabric) were applied with satin stitch blobs. The flowers are cut from pelmet interfacing, covered with satin stitch.*
VALERIE CAMPBELL-HARDING.

7 *Exploring Colour*

An isolated machine embroidery stitch is quite small and fine, although many of the textures produced on a machine may make you forget this. It gives unlimited possibilities for using pointillism – dots of different colours used together to give one effect when viewed closely and a very different colour effect when seen from a distance. Think of machine stitches as dots or fine lines of colour. Then think of how you can use them to change the colour or tone of parts of the fabric, or to blend one colour into another.

Here are some ways of doing this:

- Straight stitching in one direction, with rows of stitching quite close together or with varied spacing.
- Straight stitching in two or three directions, i.e. cross hatching.
- Straight stitching with a slightly tight top tension, so that the colour of the bobbin thread comes up. Keep changing the colour of the bobbin thread.
- Straight stitching using more than one colour in the needle. Keep changing one of the colours.
- Zigzag stitching in one direction, overlapping rows of colour.
- Zigzag in two or more directions, i.e. cross hatching.
- Freely stitched patterns, such as circles or vermicelli, which can be spaced out or overlapped to give less or more colour.

Any of these suggestions can be varied by working them over applied pieces of fabric, scraps of translucent fabric, or chopped up or meandering threads. Experiment with laying swirls of a fine rayon thread all over the surface of the fabric and using one of the ideas above, to see how it alters the colour effect.

Fabric printing and painting are often used for subtle colour changes on fabric, to indicate shadows or to change the tone of the background across an area. The techniques suggested here are not intended to take the place of printing and painting, but to add another dimension. Use both methods together. Work through the list above, stitching on your own space-dyed or printed fabrics. One lovely idea would be to stitch on a plain fabric to alter the colour of it in parts. Then spray, sponge or streak fabric paint into the stitched areas to change it further. Of course, even more stitching may then be required.

Colour experiments

We have given some ideas for blending the colour of the stitch with the colour of the fabric to produce tonal changes. Within areas of stitching, equally interesting colour effects can be produced.

Work in bands or squares of solid free running stitch – something will happen at the edges, something different in the middle and one idea will most certainly lead to another. This is the exciting part. Most of the following ideas for experiments are based on mixing two or more colours together within an area. This is a more subtle approach than changing continually from one solid colour to another. Colour mixing can generally be achieved in two ways – by the use of two colours in the needle, or by allowing the bobbin thread to show on the surface and combine with the colour of the top thread. Try the following experiments.

Primary colours

Start by using the three primary colours, red, yellow and blue. Many workers shy away from these, but

at its most intense,
re colour works will
subtle effects.

ds, using free

in the needle and

ier in the needle and

ther in the needle

ittle to bring up more
so try to control this
e and how slowly you
bbin colour build up
stitching.
yellow fabrics
ins the blue, stitch
to, or in the same
a red thread on the blue
seam line. Then use blue
thread in the same way on the red fabric. Where
the blue and yellow fabrics join, stitch blue on the
yellow and yellow on the blue. This results in a
most attractive, multi-coloured band of the
primaries, both in fabric and thread. If the stitching
is not too dense, the fabric colour will show
through the stitching, giving an optical mix of the
two.

- Choose your favourite primary colour.
  (a) Use the primary and black in the needle
  together.
  (b) Use the primary and white in the needle
  together.
  (c) Use the primary and grey in the needle
  together.
  These techniques result in tints, tones and shades
  of the colour, and would be effective used
  together in a piece of work. Use pure colour and,
  say, the pure colour and black, to shade an area
  of your design.

Complementaries

Colours which are opposite each other on the
colour circle are known as complementaries. When
used together, red and green (for example) will

appear to be a bronze/brown colour from a distance
but speckled, bright red and green close up. Try:

- Red and green in the needle together.
- Blue and orange in the needle together.
- Yellow and violet in the needle together.

Shaded and variegated threads

These are wonderful for colour experiments. Choose
a strong mix of colours in a variegated thread,
winding two bobbins with it. Put one bobbin on the
spool pin with the reel of thread on top. Thread the
two together through the needle, using the second
bobbin underneath. A more subtle colour mix will
be achieved than the same thread used on its own.

A black and white shaded thread is available. Use:

- A primary colour plus black/white together in the
  needle.
- Your favourite colour plus black/white together in
  the needle.
- A variegated thread plus black/white together in
  the needle.

Then try using the black/white thread alone in the
needle with a colour on the bobbin. Finally change
round, putting the colour on the top and the
black/white thread underneath.

Metallic threads

Use a metallic thread with every colour you possess.
Some of the nicest effects come from using:

- A metallic thread through the needle and a colour
  underneath.
  (The metallic will be speckled with the bobbin
  colour, especially at the end of a row of stitching,
  if you allow the bobbin colour to build up.)
- A coloured variegated metallic thread with one of
  its colours used in the bobbin.

We hope you will use these suggestions to add
another dimension to your embroidery. No doubt
you will have your own favourite combinations and
will think of many more to try.

8 | *Combining Different Stitches*

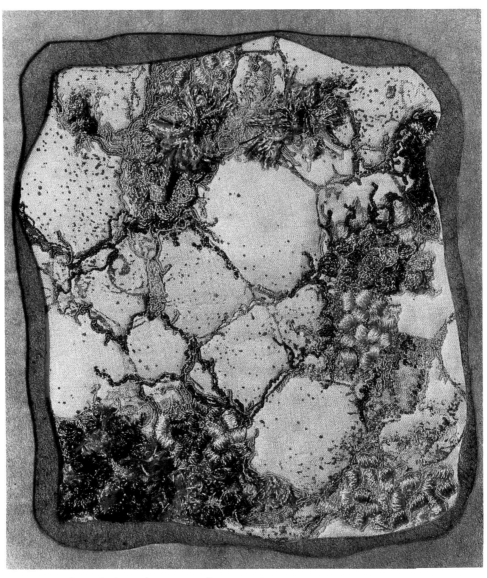

162 *'Paved Garden'. A photocopy of a bubble print was transferred to silk fabric using white spirit and a hot iron. A variety of stitches were used, including running and whip stitch, areas of looping and satin stitch blobs.* PAMELA WATTS.

The real enjoyment of machine embroidery comes when you know you can choose and put together different stitch techniques to create exactly what is in your imagination. Line, shape, pattern and texture can all be worked and it is the combination of these elements that forms the basis of exciting design. There will be surprises – the way one stitch looks next to another, a new thread or forgetting to change the tensions back to normal – and these findings are the best part of the craft. Always keep samples or notes to remind you of what happened and why. Work through a number of stitch combinations,

163 *Transfer-printed trees, with machine satin and whip stitch, and applied burnt nylon organza, are mounted in triangular shapes on a transfer-printed canvas background.* CELIA STANLEY.

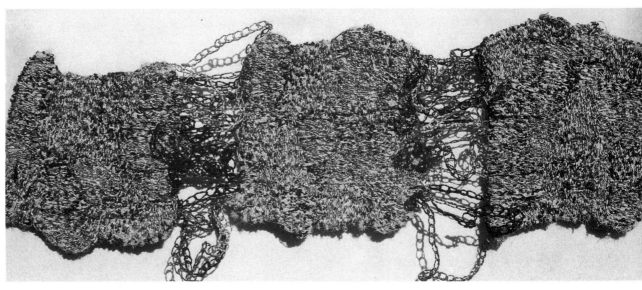

164 Above *Detail of a belt constructed of small squares of felt, with lines of chain stitch worked over the spaces between the squares. Very solid free running stitch* covers *the felt shapes, using gold metallic thread on the spool and a variegated thread on the bobbin.*

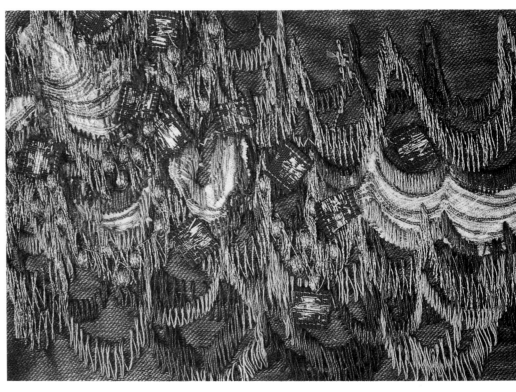

165 Above *A rich surface built up using zigzag stitching, cut pieces of ribbon, satin stitch blobs and pieces of a paler fabric decorated with whip stitch scallops, cut out and reapplied.*

166 Right *A necklace combining marbling on gold leather, organza, plastic and Jap gold threads, with areas of free running, satin and whip stitch.*
JULIE SMITH.

167 *Stitching on a fabric made by machine knitting using gold machine thread. Zigzag, satin stitch blobs and knots of ribbons give a rich texture.*

keeping to a simple one-colour scheme to begin with, so that you can fully appreciate the contrast of the textures.

- Zigzag freely over the fabric and then work areas of cable or whip stitch patterns on top.
- Work an area of close lines, varying between satin stitch of different widths, cable stitch and looping.
- Free solid running stitch with added satin stitch blobs or crosses.
- Irregularly spaced lines of running whip stitch with short lines of satin stitch superimposed.
- Close circles of free running or whip stitch combined with eyelets and circles of feather stitch.

You will guess that the list is endless and it is worthwhile to experiment as much as you can. Your own favourite combinations will emerge. Look at sketches and photographs of gardens and you will see they provide all the inspiration needed for combining stitches. It can be a literal interpretation or purely an impression of shapes, areas and colours. Either way, contrast the textures of mosses and foliage with areas of flowers or tall waving stems. Take the trouble to keep changing thread colours in order to achieve subtle tonal variations – even changing from a shiny to a matt thread of the same colour is well worth the effort. If an area does not seem quite right, work another colour into it or go over part with another stitch.

168 *Dyed strips of silk in the colours of a Cornish landscape applied with straight machine stitching and free zigzag in metallic threads.* TONI BEYNON.

169 *Right 'Conservatory'. Painted architectural patterns and embroidered satin foliage and flowers worked on acetate.* PADDY KILLER.

Combining hand and machine stitches

The majority of machine embroiderers began learning the craft as a hand technique and there is no need to abandon these skills. They combine together very well, according to the needs of the design. This is particularly useful in large-scale work, for either the church or theatre. Nowadays many of the most highly respected embroiderers combine paint, dye, hand and machine embroidery in their work. When you visit an exhibition or gallery, look closely at the exhibits and you will see that the artist has used the right technique in the right place.

There are several areas to be exploited. Many hand stitches are composite – that is, one stitch worked on a base or foundation of another. Work lines of running stitch by machine and thread through these by hand, using a tapestry needle, for Pekinese stitch or any of the threaded or whipped stitches. Change the machine stitch length, use two threads through the needle, or try a metallic thread for the base. As well as

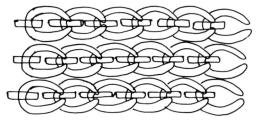

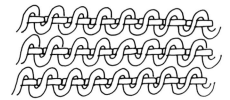

170 *Three diagrams of combined machine and hand stitching, using running or cable stitch as a base.*

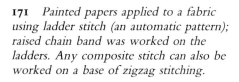

171 *Painted papers applied to a fabric using ladder stitch (an automatic pattern); raised chain band was worked on the ladders. Any composite stitch can also be worked on a base of zigzag stitching.*

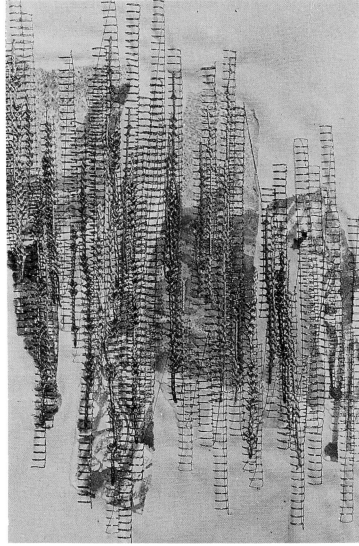

the named stitches, work a base of running stitch lines in pairs or at random and hand lace threads through, knotting and looping them as you wish. Cable stitch, too, can be used as the base for composite stitches. This reverses the idea of threading or whipping a thick thread over a thin one, as the cable will be heavy with a thin thread, perhaps metallic, threaded through by hand.

A foundation of zigzag or blanket stitch on the machine provides the base for raised chain or raised stem band. These hand stitches can also be worked

172 *'The Potting Shed'. Scraps of painted fabric and paper applied with machine free running and hand stitching. French knots, straight, cretan and detached chain stitch areas were worked. Framed with hand-made paper, burnt and painted.* MARION BROOKES.

in broken and curved lines on a freely worked area of zigzag or long tacking or basting stitches to give an irregular free effect. If your machine will do chain stitch, do try this over a drawn thread border as a raised chain band insertion. These ideas are not 'cheating'; they are valid stitches in their own right.

There are times when a piece of

embroidery needs everyone's favourite stitches – straight stitches and french knots – to add texture and direction. Try working these over free running or whip stitch and you will find that the hand and machine stitches together give extra depth to the work. Many thick threads cannot be used on the machine, even for cable stitch, so add these by hand when an extra touch of colour is needed.

Certain hand and machine stitches seem to have a natural affinity. Think of freely worked horizontal lines of zigzag with hand cretan stitch on top. Or whip stitch and bullion knots together. The two techniques, hand and machine, can be highly compatible. Consider working part of the design on the machine before adding hand stitches. Satin stitch blobs or eyelets on the machine might come next, finishing with clusters of french or bullion knots by hand.

Stitching applied to stitching

In earlier chapters on techniques we have often suggested working overlapping lines and areas of stitching, rather than single lines. Take this theme one stage further by applying pieces of machine embroidered fabric on to machine embroidery to build up layers of richness and texture. It literally adds another dimension in creating a total textile. A very good way of experimenting is to use scraps of practice stitching. Select an area of solid stitching, cut it out and apply it to another fabric which has also been machined. Stitch through both layers to integrate the edges, deciding whether to leave the appliqué flat or raised in parts. An alternative method is to decide on the shape to be applied,

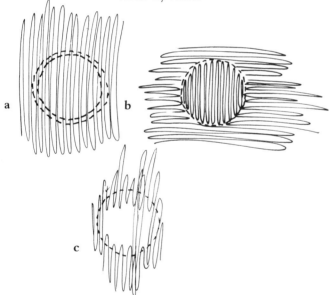

173(a) *Stitch twice around a shape on a piece of machine stitching.*
(b) *Cut it out between the lines of stitching and apply to another piece of stitching.*
(c) *Stitch over edges to integrate.*

174 *Pieces of rich stitching applied to a fabric with further stitching worked to blend it, making a raised area which looks padded. This piece is worked in running, cable and whip stitches in pinks, lilacs and gold.*

stitch twice round the shape before cutting out between the stitched lines, and then apply and stitch as before. Try small pieces at first, as they are easier to handle. With a little experience, however, large areas of a design can be treated in this way.

175 *Pieces of stitching applied to other stitching, holes cut out and stitching placed behind them, and pieces of open knitting in metal thread stiffened with PVA laid on top. Stitching was worked through all layers to integrate them.*

176, 177 Above *Bracelet and hat.*
JUDY CLAYTON.

*Judy Clayton has developed her
embroidery techniques to produce a
finished material which is light and flexible.
Exotic fabrics and threads are sandwiched
between layers of transparent plastic with
machine embroidery. A variety of softer
textures such as dyed or painted felt or
velvet are added, and then machine
embroidered, leaving part of the
background exposed.*

178 Right *Hand and machine embroidery worked on pieces of black
square mesh net which were laid on painted paper. Painted and
gilded rug canvas, with hand darning in some areas, was then laid
on top and small pieces of bright gold leather were laid behind the
canvas. The whole sandwich was laid on black net over gold lamé
and machined in areas to hold the layers together. The frame is
pelmet interfacing, painted with black fabric paint, printed with
gold paint using pieces of rug canvas, and with more gold paint
dabbed around the edges. Both the inside and outside edges were
burnt with a candle to give an irregular line.*
VALERIE CAMPBELL-HARDING.

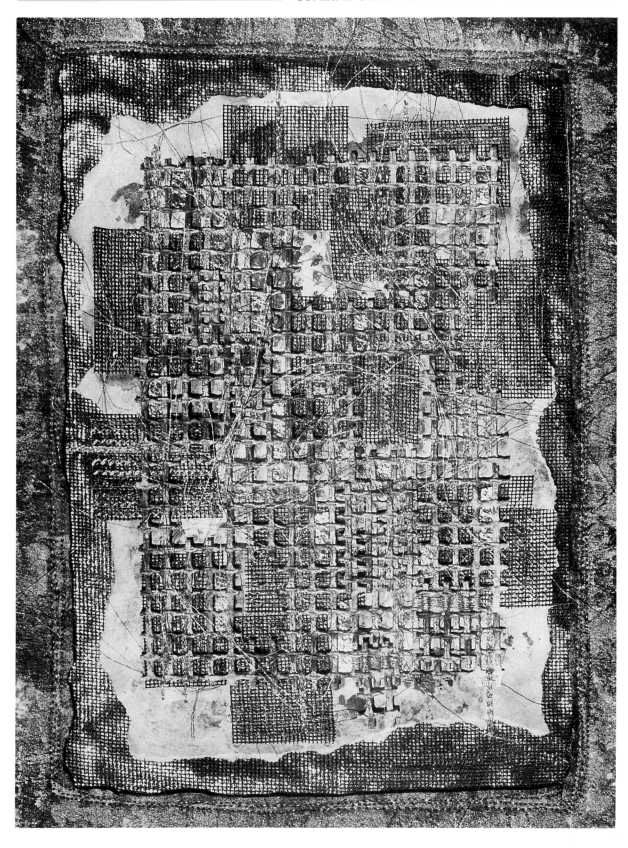

179 *A panel based on drawings of the pattern of a pineapple skin. It is made in three layers. The back layer is machining on hand-made paper. The central pieces are free-hanging, made of brightly coloured and lurex fabric, machine stitched. The front layer is pelmet interfacing, with applied lurex fabrics in some parts and irregular machining.* LINDA RAKSHIT.

180 Right *'Blue Nymph'. Solid stitching in irregular areas, with the stitching so distorting the fabric that the embroidery has a folded and undulating surface, planned to emphasize particular areas of the design.* ALICE KETTLE.

Interpreting Your Drawings and Designs

Whether you are confident or hesitant about drawing and designing for embroidery, you will find that machine embroidery makes the interpretation much easier. Consider, for a moment, the action of the machine. As you move the fabric the needle draws lines, curves and circles which look remarkably similar to the marks you would make with a pencil. This affinity between the pencil and needle should convince even the faint-hearted of the value of drawing. Another benefit is that you can allow the spontaneity of the machine to play its part in developing and adding to your drawings. Rather than just producing a carbon copy, let the machine add depth, texture and colour to your drawings. Many machine embroiderers develop a style of drawing which seems to imitate the action of the machine. Or is it the other way round? The machine imitates the artist. Keep a sketchbook by your machine and try for yourself. Draw a series of lines, wiggles, curves and circles, noticing the rhythm of the pencil. Stitch exactly the same marks on the fabric with free running stitch, remembering the feel of the rhythm. Shade an area with pencil or pen, hatching and cross-hatching, and then the same pattern of tone on the machine. Experiment further with anything that will make marks on paper. Try big wide brush marks, dragging the edge of a piece of card dipped in paint, or scratchy felt-tip pens. Look really hard at the marks and concentrate on producing the same effect on fabric with the machine. When you have seen this for yourself, your own drawings will take on new meaning. Do not restrict

181 *Stylized drawing of a landscape, in black ink.*

your interpretation to running stitch, but use the texture of whip or cable, encroaching zigzag or satin stitch to develop your drawings to new dimensions.

182 *Pencil drawing of folds of fabric, suggesting stitchery built up in layers, each layer stitched in a different direction.*

183 *A panel based on marks made with black ink, which was applied to paper by blowing with a straw, by dabbing and streaking with a sponge, by streaking with the edge of corrugated paper and by printing with crumpled paper. The design was planned and the embroidery carried out to look as much like the paint marks as possible. The stitching is on cream fabric and the embroidery pieces are window-mounted within the paper design.*
LESLEY IRVING.

184 *A design achieved by placing strips of paper over a drawing to give areas of restfulness against the detail. This style of drawing strongly suggests machine stitchery, and the varying tones and directions give liveliness.* VAL DU CROS.

185 Right *A detail from the final embroidery. The fabric was first painted freely to suggest petals and leaves. Small pieces of transparent fabric, net and machine-made lace (worked on water-soluble fabric) were applied, and free running and whip stitch worked over them.* VAL DU CROS.

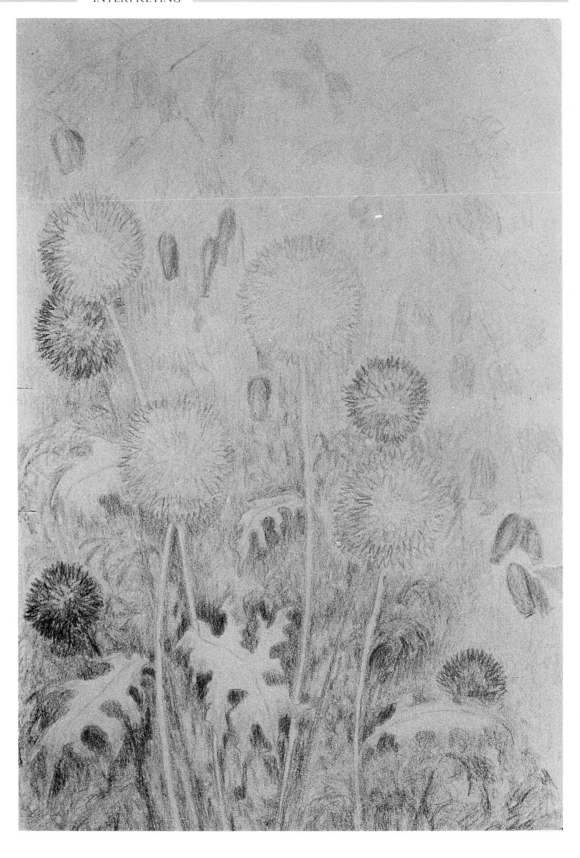

186 Left *A multi-coloured drawing of a flower garden using coloured pencil. The directions of the pencil marks are important, as are the spaces and voided lines.* JOAN ABBOTT.

187 *A first trial using free running stitch in many coloured threads. This could be developed using different stitch lengths and directions on different fabrics to see the results. The stitchery in this type of embroidery needs to be as subtle and well drawn as the original.* JOAN ABBOTT.

188 *Drawings of patterns using the freely stitched flowers described on page 98.*

189 *Bands of flowers arranged with areas of textured fringing and straight stitching using varying stitch lengths.*
GILL MASTERTON-BROWN.

190 *A small piece based on a drawing in
pencil and wash and coloured pencil. The
fabric is painted and pieces of frayed fabric
are laid over some areas. Free running,*
*whip, feather and satin stitch are
used freely to give movement and texture.*
VAL DU CROS.

191 Left *A design built up from torn and burnt pieces of paper which had previously been decorated by sponging, streaking and painting. Marks were added with a flat brush. The colours are reds, golds and black, with a very rich result.*
MARIAN MURPHY.

192 *Panel based on the collage. Machine-wrapped threads are stitched together to make a grid, laid over stitching on hand-made paper. Fabrics are crumple-painted, stitched in layers and slashed. Pieces have been made by stitching across holes (page 98) and applied, and squares and rectangles applied over free satin stitching with more stitching over them, as well as ruched and stitched lamé. The colours are reds, black and golds, which give a medieval richness.* MARIAN MURPHY.

193 Left *A scraperboard design of Othello, as played by Laurence Olivier. The white scraperboard was first decorated with bubble prints in many pale colours and the design scratched through to show white against the colour.* DIANA KING.

194 *Embroidery worked from the design, after many trials and samples. The white satin was transfer printed with bubble prints, and free running and whip stitch in coloured and gold threads emphasized the patterns. Pieces of white felt were applied on the face, stitched with invisible nylon thread to give texture, yarn was applied to make the streaks and extra free running added to suggest hair. All white stitching except the hair, which is gold.* DIANA KING.

195 *A collage built up from paper designs and trials of stitching for a machine-embroidered bag. It is worth producing many different samples so that you can choose the best one for your purpose.* KAY BALL.

196 Right *The finished bag, which is mainly machining on canvas, inset with small octagons of hand-embroidered tent stitch on the same canvas. The colours blend from black through to warm golden yellow, with gold metallic threads. The central spiral and the handle are of machine-wrapped string. There are small tassels inside as a surprise, and the two small bags fit inside the larger one.* KAY BALL.

197 *A design for a pulpit fall, using a cross drawn in coloured pencil. The directions of the pencil strokes make a strong contribution. This design would be suitable for an altar frontal which requires embroidery on a much larger scale.* CHRISTINE COOK.

198 *A burse made as part of the same set, from a similar design. The background is coloured with zigzag whip stitch, and straight lines of gold stitching worked over it. The cross is of gold-painted pelmet interfacing, held down with hand stitching. The central spaces are textured with gold zigzag, free running stitch, satin stitch blobs and pieces of gold purl applied by hand.* CHRISTINE COOK.

Troubleshooting

It is reassuring that the majority of problems in machine embroidery can be avoided or easily solved.

Care of your machine

Do read your manual, especially the 'Care and maintenance' section, and make a friend of your machine dealer. If there is something 'not quite right' with your machine, or if it needs servicing, do have it attended to right away. Small irritations in ordinary sewing can become big problems in embroidery. Make a habit of cleaning your machine regularly, especially around the bobbin area. Fluff should be brushed out, and tiny pieces of thread caught in the race can be removed with tweezers if necessary. Oil the race: only a drop is required, but check in the manual for specific instructions. Keep your machine in a warm room. Like cars, machines do not perform very well when cold. If you are going to a class, do not put your machine in the car the night before. You should also never transport your machine on its side, as the motor oil can leak. We always wedge ours securely upright in the boot or on the passenger seat – with a safety belt on, of course.

Top thread breaking

This seems to be the most common, and the most annoying, problem. Check through all the following points:

- Top tension too tight – loosen, little by little, until breaking stops.
- Thread old or brittle – wind off the top layer, or steam over boiling water. (Threads should be stored in a covered container.) Use a new thread, if possible.
- Thread caught on the base of the spool pin – read 'Using tricky threads' in the Introduction.
- Try a larger needle size.
- Use a darning foot.
- Tighten the fabric in the frame.

Remember that loosening the tension may not help if the thread is old or the fabric loose in the frame.

Missed stitches

- Fabric not tight enough in the frame – most likely cause.
- Bent or blunt needle – use a new one regularly.
- Machine not threaded properly – check again.
- Needle too small – change to a larger size.
- Use a darning foot.

Needle breaks

- Needle not inserted as high as it should be.
- Needle bent, probably caused by pulling the frame away from the machine.
  Support the needle with your finger when you remove the work. Your frame may be a tight fit under the needle, causing it to catch on, and bend, the needle. Always remember to raise the needle to its highest position, and try to get a thinner frame.

Loops of top thread underneath

- If continuous – you have left the presser foot up.
- Occasional – probably a loose thread caught in the race.

Unusual noises

You will become very familiar with the normal noise of your machine running. If you hear anything unusual, however slight, stop stitching at once and try to identify the problem. Be convinced that if will never 'clear itself' if you keep going. It will just take even longer to unravel the race.

In conclusion

If a problem occurs, try not to get flustered, changing everything you can think of. Work through the possibilities, one at a time. Perhaps you had a good idea and rushed to the machine to try it out. The thread breaks, loops appear when you had not wanted them and, before long, both you and your machine are hot and bothered. Relax, sit comfortably and try to get the feel of the rhythm of the machine.

What to Look For When Choosing a Sewing Machine

If you are fortunate enough to buy a sewing machine with machine embroidery in mind, the following list may give you some ideas of what to look for. You may not find all these points in the model you are considering, but decide for yourself which are most important to *you*.

- You should be able to drop the feed dog. Some machines have a cover plate which works adequately, but this reduces the space in which to insert an embroidery frame.
- When the presser foot has been removed (and, on some machines, the short connecting shank) there should be enough space under it, and also under the needle at its highest point, to insert a frame.
- You should be able to alter the tensions of both the top and the bobbin threads easily.
- The machine should stop *instantly* when you remove your foot from the pedal, not go on for a couple of stitches.
- The metal plate covering the bobbin and race should be flush with the bed of the machine so that your embroidery frame will not catch on it.

- The needle should be positioned in the centre of the free arm, not towards the back or the front, as this causes the frame to tip.
- A needle 'stop up' and 'stop down' facility is useful – but you need *both*, or *neither* (you can then learn to control the foot pedal to achieve this).
- The machine should sew slowly enough to give you complete control of what you are doing. One stitch at a time is useful.
- You must be able to graduate the width of the stitch smoothly, not in steps.
- You must be able to control the stitch length from 0–5 within very fine limits – again, not in steps.
- Look for a nice big bobbin that does not need continual refilling.
- If possible, the bobbins should fit on the spool pin so that you can use more than two threads at a time. This is also convenient for working with tricky threads wound on to a bobbin and used on top of the spool pin.

Further Reading

Some of these books are out of print, but you may be able to find them at your local library.

Books on machine embroidery
Anne Butler, *Machine Stitches,* Batsford
Joy Clucas, *The New Machine Embroidery,* David and Charles
Anne Coleman, *The Creative Sewing Machine,* Batsford
Jennifer Gray, *Machine Embroidery: Technique and Design,* Batsford
Moyra McNeill, *Machine Embroidery: Lace and See-Through Techniques,* Batsford
Christine Risley, *Machine Embroidery,* Studio Vista
Verina Warren, *Landscape in Embroidery,* Batsford

Books for inspiration
Andreas Feininger, *Nature Close-Up,* Dover
Angela Fisher, *Africa Adorned,* Collins
Lehndorff and Trulzsch, *Verushka,* Thames and Hudson
Maxine Masterman, *Painting the Spirit of Nature,* Watson Guptill
Monet's Years at Giverny, Metropolitan Museum of Art, New York
Georges Meurant, *Shoowa Design – African Textiles from the Kingdom of Kuba,*
    Thames and Hudson
Roger Phillips, *Grasses, Ferns, Mosses and Lichens of Great Britain and Ireland*
    Pan Books Ltd
G. T. Prance, *Leaves,* Thames and Hudson
Charles Sheffield, *Earthwatch,* Sidgwick and Jackson

Suppliers

UK

Sewing machine manufacturers

Bernina Sewing Machines,
Bogod House, 50–52 Great Sutton Street,
London EC1V 0DJ

Elna Sewing Machines (GB) Ltd,
180–182 Tottenham Court Road,
London W1P 9LE

Frister and Rossman Sewing Machines Ltd,
Mark Way, Swanley, Kent BR8 8NQ

Jones Sewing Machine Co. Ltd,
Shepley Street, Guide Bridge,
Audenshaw, Manchester M34 5JD

New Home Sewing Machine Co. Ltd,
Cromwell Road, Bredbury,
Stockport, Cheshire SK6 2SH

Viking-Husqvarna Ltd,
PO Box 10, Oakley Road,
Luton LU4 9QW

Threads

All these firms offer a mail order service.

Campden Needlecraft Centre,
High Street, Chipping Campden,
Gloucestershire

Mace and Nairn,
89 Crane Street, Salisbury, Wiltshire

Needle and Thread,
80 High Street, Horsell,
Woking, Surrey

Shades,
57 Candlemas Lane, Beaconsfield,
Buckinghamshire

Silken Strands,
33 Linksway, Gatley, Cheadle,
Cheshire SK8 4LA

Fabrics

Borovicks,
16 Berwick Street, London W1

Liberty and Co.
Regent Street, London W1

MacCulloch and Wallis,
25–26 Dering Street, London W1R 0BH

George Weil and Sons,
63–65 Riding House Street,
London W1P 7PP

Whaleys (Bradford) Ltd,
Harris Court, Great Horton,
Bradford, West Yorkshire BD7 4EQ

Out-of-print books

Doreen Gill,
14 Barnfield Road, Petersfield,
Hampshire GU31 4DQ

Judith Mansfield,
60a Dornton Road, London SW12 9NE

Sacketts,
34 Dorset Street, Blandford Forum, Dorset

Thomas Thorpe,
170 High Street, Guildford,
Surrey GU1 3HP

New difficult-to-obtain and foreign books

Neil Davies,
Crafts of Quality Books,
1 Wingrad House, Jubilee Street,
London E1 3BJ

USA

Sewing machine manufacturers

Larson Bernina Corporation,
2017 East 78 Street, Minneapolis 55401

White Sewing Machine Co.
11750 Berea Road, Cleveland, Ohio 44111
(Elna machines)

Mail order embroidery supplies

Aardvark Adventure,
Box 2449, Livermore, Ca 94550

American Handicrafts,
2617 W. Seventh Street,
Fort Worth, Texas

The Counting House at the
Hammock Shop,
Box 155, Pawley Island,
South Carolina, 29585

Peters Valley Craftsmen
Layton, New Jersey, 07851

Many chain stores also stock embroidery
supplies. For local specialist shops, see
Yellow Pages.

Index

applied stitching 26, 86, 97, 105, 112–119, 120, 122
applique 11–13, 18, 27, 35, 82, 93, 107, 114, 121, 126, 133, 135, 166
automatic patterns 48, 54, 70, 88–92, 94, 116

backgrounds, stitched, 23–25, 33, 42, 63
bobbin, hand winding the, 55
breaking threads 140
buttonholes 86, 87

cable stitch 52–59
canvas, stitching on 84, 105, 121, 136, 137
care of the machine 8
choosing a machine 142
colours 108, 109
corners 77
couching 26, 27, 62, 63
cutwork 80, 81

darning foot 21
drawn fabric 72
drawn thread 71, 90
drawing 124–130, 138
distortion 100, 101, 123

edges 28, 29, 78, 79, 99
eyelets 94, 106, 107

fabrics 7, 10, 28–30, 45, 64, 66, 67, 76, 78, 79, 95
failure, what to do with a, 12
feather stitch 50, 51, 131

free cable stitch 56–59
free running 16–18, 20, 32, 35, 95, 96, 98, 112, 118, 120, 127, 131, 135, 139
free satin stitch 83–85
free zigzag 61, 63
fringing 99, 130

hand stitching 48, 84, 116, 117, 121, 139

insertions 73

landscapes 34, 44, 62, 99, 103, 104
long stitches 84, 102, 103, 105
looping foot 72–74, 110

magic needle 102
making a fabric 29, 96
making a thread 68–70, 74, 102, 133, 137
massed stitching 8, 12, 13, 15, 18, 24, 25, 35, 36, 38, 42, 43, 48, 93, 100–102, 112, 120, 123
metal threads 7, 27, 36, 41, 53, 77, 87, 101, 104, 107, 109, 137, 139
moss stitch 49

needles 6
needles, twin 14, 15, 70

preparing the machine 8

quilting 15, 16, 22, 24, 25

running, free 16–18, 20, 21, 35, 95, 96, 112, 118, 120, 127, 131, 135,139

running stitch 9, 139

satin stitch 47, 60, 75–90, 94, 105, 110, 112, 114, 115, 131
satin stitch, padded 85
slashing 16
stabilizers 10
starting a thread 18
stitching across space 55, 98, 99, 130, 133
stitching in different directions 11
stitching, massed 8, 12, 13, 15, 18, 24, 25, 35, 36, 38, 42, 43, 48, 93, 100–102, 112, 120, 123
stitching on canvas 84, 105, 121, 136, 137
stitching on mesh 96
stitching to distort 100, 101

tailor-tacking foot 72–74, 100
tensions 19, 34, 52, 61, 75
threads 7–9, 13, 36, 52, 53, 76, 109
troubleshooting 140
twin needles 14, 15, 70

vermicelli 19, 32, 33

water-soluble fabrics 28–30, 32, 93, 107
whip stitch 38–49, 103, 110, 112, 135, 139
wrapping 68–70, 133, 137

zigzag, sideways 104
zigzag stitch 54, 60–74, 106, 112, 114